Dark Peak Aircraft Wrecks 2

Dark Peak Aircraft Wrecks 2

Ron Collier

LEO COOPER
LONDON

First published in 1982 by
Wharncliffe Publishing Limited.

Republished in this edition 1992, by
LEO COOPER Ltd
190 Shaftesbury Avenue, London WC2H 8JL
an imprint of Pen & Sword Books Ltd
47 Church Street, Barnsley, S. Yorkshire S70 2AS

Reprinted 1995

Copyright © Ron Collier, 1982, 1992, 1995

*For up-to date information on other titles produced under
the Leo Cooper imprint, please telephone or write to:*

Pen & Sword Books Ltd
FREEPOST
47 Church Street
Barnsley
South Yorkshire S70 2BR
Telephone (24 hours): 01226 734555

ISBN: 0 85052 336 2

A CIP catalogue record of this book is available
from the British Library

Printed in Great Britain by
Redwood Books Limited
Trowbridge, Wiltshire

Contents

ACCESS TO OPEN COUNTRY

Seventy-six square miles of the moorlands of the Peak District are open to the public through access agreements between the Peak National Park Joint Planning Board and the owners of the land. This is subject to certain conditions: the Board's by-laws and closure up to twelve days in the grouse-shooting season (12th August to 10th December inclusive).

All the aircraft wrecks in this publication are on private land and permission is required from individual landowners to dig at these sites. If permission is not sought and a person is seen to be digging, an offence may be committed (maximum penalty, £400 or six month's imprisonment, or both).

MINISTRY OF DEFENCE

Military aircraft that crash in the United Kingdom remain the property of the Crown, along with any equipment, until such time as the Ministry of Defence decides to dispose of them.

Crashed enemy aircraft (German) and equipment found in the United Kingdom are regarded as captured enemy property that has been surrendered to the Crown.

Crashed American military aircraft remain the property of the United States government, but the Ministry of Defence acts on behalf of the United States authorities.

Any group wishing to recover the wreckage of military aircraft should first approach the following authority before proceeding:

The Ministry of Defence Air Force Board Secretariat
Room 8239
Main Building
Whitehall
London SW1A 2HB

WARNING

The moors of the Peak District are on mountains, and in bad weather, which can occur at any time, they can be dangerous. Adequate clothing plus map and compass should be carried at all times. It is advisable to inform someone of where you intend to go, and then stick to your declared route.

For **MOUNTAIN RESCUE** *telephone 999; for the* **POLICE OPERATIONS ROOM** *telephone 0773 43551.*

PHILLIP SHAW *Glossop*

This book is dedicated to the memory of my dear friend and constant walking companion, Ken Kershaw, whose original idea it was. Ken was killed by lightning, Sunday, 1st May, 1988, whilst hill-walking on Caer Cardoc, Shropshire.

Acknowledgments

To produce a work of this nature requires the co-operation of many people. The following names are of those individuals who have kindly contributed, in some measure, to the compilation of this record whether by the loan of photographs, supply of information and documents, or giving of their time in other ways. Ron Collier could not begin his acknowledgments without first making mention of his wife, Susan. Susan, it must be said, has not the slightest interest in aeroplanes — and when it comes to aircraft archaeology, she is the first to admit that she doesn't know the difference between an oleo leg and a radial engine. This has not, however, prevented her from supporting her husband in his interests; she has helped him with exhibitions and slide lectures, and played hostess to numerous aircraft crash survivors, who have visited their home. All of that, when Susan's own interests include pottery and hand-painted china — a far cry from the aviation relics that occupy so much of her husband's time and resources.

Some of the individuals and organisations who have made this work on aviation history possible:

Acton E, ex-Army Bomb Disposal; Air Data Publications; Allonby T, aviation historian; Bancroft K; Beacham Brooker, ex-4 Fighter Group; Biddulph F, Squadron Leader, ex-102 Squadron; Bishop S, USAAF historian; Blunt B, researcher and writer; Buckley P Mrs; Burk V, 3rd Air Force historian; Cartwright H, ex-150 Squadron; Carter E Miss; Chappell J, Holmfirth ATC; Connatty P, loss lists and initial information; Coyle, Captain, 427 Squadron historian; Coulson Mrs, Canada; Crichton Doctor, Air Commodore, Mountain Rescue Service, retired; Davies J, retired railwayman, Crowden; Freeman R, 8th Air Force historian; Frith D, historian; Graham G, ex-150 Squadron; Hamer J, ex-searchlight unit, Edale; Herdman F, Mrs, Edale; Hodgkiss P, aviation historian; Holmes H, 8th Air Force historian; Ives R, aviation historian; Jones A, artist; Lawton M, photographs; Mason J, gamekeeper; Matthews W, New Zealand; Merrick K, author; Nitschke L, ex-4 Fighter Group; Oates M, Edale; O'Connell J, ex-police special constable, Meltham; Otter V C, Air Vice Marshall, ex-102 Squadron; Ownsworth J, aviation historian; Price J, ex-150 Squadron; Quill P, Mrs, New Zealand; Reynolds I, ex-427 Squadron, Canada; Robinson B, archivist; Rouse; Russell W, USA; Shaw P, Mountain Rescue Team; Sidwell L, 7 Squadron historian; Smith D, aviation historian/author; Smith, Peter J C, author of *Flying Bombs Over the Pennines*, published by Neil Richardson; Stevens B, aviation historian; Ritchie J, ex-96 Squadron; Simpson J M; Stovell A; Sutcliffle C, Ashton-under-Lyne reporter; Tasker F, Meltham; Taylor B, retired schoolmaster; Townsend J, ex-gamekeeper; Utton W, Mossley; Wake, Air Commodore, ex-166 Squadron; Villiers P, Wing Commander, ex-102 Squadron; Ward H, ex-radio operator, Ringway; Weldon A, ex-150 Squadron.

ACCIDENT INVESTIGATION BRANCH DEPARTMENT OF TRADE, Caseley V G S; 28 MAINTENANCE UNIT MOUNTAIN RESCUE TEAM: Austin C, Squadron Leader Fitton K, Heywood S, Parks W, Pritchard D; MINISTRY OF DEFENCE NAVAL HISTORICAL BRANCH, Brown J; PUBLIC RECORDS OFFICE, Lambert F F; POLISH AIR FORCE ASSOCIATION 2nd AIR DIVISION NEWSLETTER, Editor Robertie W; AIR FORCE RELATIONS OFFICER ROYAL NEW ZEALAND AIR FORCE Squadron Leader Lumsden K; 1196 SQUADRON ATC, officers, staff and cadets 1965-1979.

Directors and staff of the following organisations: AIR MINISTRY CASUALTY BRANCH; OFFICERS' RECORDS; AIRMEN'S RECORDS; AUSTRALIAN RECORDS; CANADIAN RECORDS; AIR HISTORICAL BRANCH MINISTRY OF DEFENCE, Turner E H; IMPERIAL WAR MUSEUM, Hines E.

For help in locating crash sites: Winterbottom N; Scarrett G; Cox B and members of the GLOSSOP & PEAK DISTRICT AIRCRAFT ARCHAEOLOGY SOCIETY.

The following for special assistance: Padley J, Mrs, secretary and typist; THE BARNSLEY CHRONICLE for writing and publishing the accounts in their Group of newspapers, and producing the books; Oakley S, Mrs, for checking the text and Toby Buchan for editing and suggesting final corrections.

Finally, Kershaw K, for suggesting the book in the first place. Ken was killed by lightning May 1st, 1988, whilst hill walking. Both Dark Peak Aircraft Wrecks books One and Two are dedicated to his memory.

Without a doubt it was one of the most disastrous days that the RAF had experienced in peacetime. Seven twin-engined bi-planes of 102 Squadron had set out from Aldergrove, in Northern Ireland, to return to their base at RAF Finningley on the morning of 12th December, 1936 — only one arrived safely.

The Handley Page Heyfords, each carrying a crew of four, had taken off at 10.45 in perfect weather conditions. Flying in loose V formation they crossed the Irish Sea, passing over the English coast at Barrow-in-Furness. Before them was a huge cloud mass of icy fog.

Fully expecting the clouds to disperse as they flew inland, the crews pressed on into the 'clag'. Immediately ice began to form on the wings and control of the bombers became more difficult. Leading the formation, Squadron Leader Attwood was unable to keep the bombers together as each individual Heyford was swallowed up in the murk. From then on it became a struggle for each pilot to save himself and his crew.

For some time the ungainly machines roared on looking for possible landing places, while falling petrol gauges spelt danger to watchful pilots.

Sergeant Biddulph, after much difficulty, located Finningley and made a perfect landing through the murk. A worried reception committee waited to greet the crew of the lone bomber. The sergeant pilot thought that he was the last to land, and that he would be in trouble for getting in late — he was the only one out of seven to arrive safely.

As Biddulph taxied towards the hangers six air dramas were being played out in different parts of the country.

Sergeant Williams in Heyford K4864 crash-landed at Gainsborough — he and his crew were down safely. Heyford K5188, piloted by Flying Officer Gyll Murray, force-landed near York, and they too were unhurt. Squadron Leader Attwood, in K4868, circled a field at Jackson Edge, Disley, close by the boundary of the Peak District. Keeping close to his leader was Pilot Officer Clifford in K6898.

Attwood brought off a perfect landing in the small field and the crew scrambled out to watch as Clifford attempted a landing close by. On the

Heyford K4874 flown by Pat Villiers about to enter the cloud bank that would bring down six of the seven aircraft belonging to 102 squadron. *FROM A PAINTING BY ALAN JONES*

Flight Lieutenant Pat Villiers

second attempt Clifford's Heyford tore through some fencing, touched down, smashed through a set of iron railings, ripped up a telegraph pole and came to rest with its nose in a shrubbery. The crew climbed out of the shattered up bomber unharmed.

Nosing its way through the murk over Hebden Bridge was K6900, piloted by Sergeant Otter. The crew were peering down trying to get their bearings as the bomber skimmed low over the chimney pots. A mile from the town the machine struck a low wall and ploughed its way up a steep rutted hillside, where it burst into flames, killing three of the crew. Sergeant Otter escaped with his life.

K4874 was in difficulty over Oldham as it circled around for half an hour before crashing in the yard of Dingle Farm, at the northern edge of the Peak District. Minutes before the crash Flight Lieutenant Pat Villiers had ordered his crew to jump. Then, with ice building up on the control surfaces, he trimmed the aircraft as best he could, made his way down the fuselage to the lower mid-turret aperture and dropped out into the swirling, icy mist. Apart from him breaking a leg on landing, both he and his crew got off lightly.

At the court of inquiry that followed, pack ice forming on aircraft surfaces was blamed for the disaster. It was agreed that conditions like it had never been experienced before.

Conditions like those experienced by the pilots of 102 Squadron were to be encountered by many more pilots in the next decade, as the war years brought about a tremendous increase in flying activity over this country's high ground. Over fifty aircraft crashed in the Dark Peak area alone, in many instances leaving wreckage that remains to this day.

The question is often asked as to the likelihood of there being undiscovered aircraft on the moors. Whilst it is most unlikely, there always remains the possibility. There are still areas of moorland that rarely see a hiker, rock climber, or gamekeeper — areas that are so laced with bogs that no one would go there for pleasure. It is in these areas, far from the recognised paths, that the remains of an aircraft could lie undiscovered, embedded deep in the peat.

In the late nineteen-sixties a shepherd in the Highlands of Scotland one day noticed something sticking out of the ground. It turned out to be the wreckage of a Wellington bomber which had been given up for lost over the North Sea during the war. Although he had been in that particular area on many previous occasions, he had been totally unaware of its existence.

FROM A PAINTING BY ALAN JONES

Hampden LA055, 83 Squadron RAF, returning to Scampton from a raid on the German railway system in the area of Munchen-Gladbach, crashed near Holmfirth, 23rd May, 1940.

Map reference 098058 ● Map key number 26

They were desperate days. The 'phoney war' of the autumn and winter of '39 had ended with the invasion of Holland and Belgium in the spring of 1940. That initial surge of German forces into the Lowlands of Europe, had not not been unexpected by the British and French — it took place on Friday 10th May, 1940.

Allied counter-action, planned for just such an attack, called for an advance into Belgium to hold what they considered to be the main thrust into the north. When the British Expeditionary Force, along with the cream of the French Army, moved into Belgium they had fallen into a trap. Hitler's northern invasion was not the main thrust, but was a diversionary move. The main attack came through the wooded hills of the Ardennes and, within a mere eleven days, elements of Army Group 'A' under von Rundstedt had reached the Channel. The Allied forces were cut in two and the BEF was falling back on the Channel port of Dunkirk.

The French insisted on support from RAF Bomber Command, and the British Army too called for help against the mighty Blitzkrieg machine that was sweeping them back towards the sea.

Supplies and communications were to be the target for the British bombers. On 22nd May, 1940, twenty-eight airmen, making up the crews of seven Hampdens of 83 Squadron, Scampton, were briefed for a raid that night.

At the disposal of the advancing Germans was a vast railway network, which was busy carrying supplies and reinforcements to the frontier. Although daylight raids were proving too costly in aircraft brought down by flak and fighters, night attacks on rail communications could prove mildly successful.

The code name for attacks upon road and rail targets was 'Ploughing Operations — roving'. Hampdens of 83 Squadron were to attempt to strafe trains moving westwards towards France. One of the pilots at that briefing was Guy Gibson, later to become famous as the leader of the Dam Busters. In his book *Enemy Coast Ahead* he recalls those early days.

"Things were going badly in Belgium and France, but over in England fog came up regularly as if by the will of God to cover our fields and prevent us from operating."

Confirming the conditions of that period in 1940 is Mr Stan Harpham, who was also present with Guy Gibson at that briefing on 22nd May. Stan Harpham, pilot of Hampden L4057, recalled: "That night the weather was hopeless — overcast and hazy."

Also at that briefing was a crew that had been brought together especially for the raid on Hitler's trains — the crew of Hampden L4055. It would prove to be their first and last mission together.

In those early days of World War II there was a great deal of trial and error involved in bombing operations; early raids on Germany bordered upon the haphazard. Crews could choose their own routes to and from the target area; they could unload their bombs from whichever height they preferred. Take-off time alone was decided for them.

In the words of another crewman present at that briefing, the then AC1 Ted Sayers, wireless operator/air gunner on Hampden L4058: "We were all beginners really — there was nothing to be done about it . . . one just got stuck in and learned about things as they happened — the hard way."

Against this background, the crew of the ill-fated L4055 could be considered experienced. The pilot, Sergeant Jenkins, and air gunner, Sergeant Marsh, had flown seven previous missions. For A/C Willie Thornton it was to be his first and last mission as wireless operator. Sergeant Peter Josse was the navigator — it was his third sortie, although on those

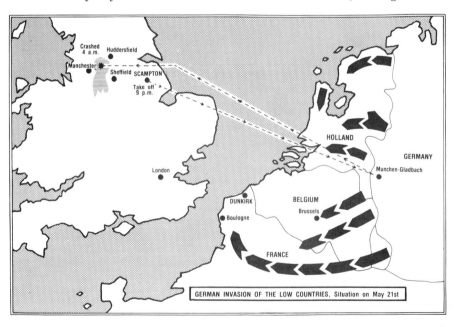

GERMAN INVASION OF THE LOW COUNTRIES, Situation on May 21st

two previous occasions he had flown as air gunner. He was no novice when it came to navigation, for he had twelve years' peace-time service in the RAF, serving in Amman with 14 Squadron and in Egypt with 6 Squadron. By the standards of the day, he could be regarded as an experienced man.

It was dusk as the Hampden bombers of 83 Squadron moved from their dispersal points at Scampton. Each turned into the wind — then, at five-minute intervals, they took off from the grass field and headed towards Holland.

L4055 was the first away at 9 o'clock; Guy Gibson in L4070 was the last up at 9.30 pm. Seven bombers were heading for targets close to Germany's border with Holland.

Radiating from the area of Munchen-Gladbach was a railway system that was important to the success of the German invasion. The Hampden crews were to seek out and bomb targets leading from that rail centre to the front.

Over Europe the weather was against them, yet despite that, five crews located targets and attacked with varying degrees of success. Squadron-Leader Field caught two trains in a station at Gelden and destroyed both of them. Flight-Lieutenant Collier and his crew attacked a train near the German town of Emmerich, but were unable to observe the results. They released a remaining bomb over the aerodrome at Upenburg. Goods trains standing on tracks near the town of Hasselt were caught by Pilot-Officer Lyster and direct hits were observed. Bursting flak peppered their aircraft with shrapnel and AC1 Sayers, in the upper rear turret position, lost the right heel of his flying boot — but there were no injuries.

Pilot-Officer Bird and his crew made the longest flight that night, arriving over Neuss-Gruenbroich where they spotted two trains, which they immediately tried to bomb. No results were

Sergeant Stanley Jenkins, pilot

seen and they climbed into the overcast and headed home for Scampton.

Last to have got into the air and the last to leave the target area was Guy Gibson in a labouring L4070. A railway bridge over the Schelde-Mass Canal was lined up in the bomb-sight by Pilot-Officer Watson, who lay cramped up in the nose. As they climbed away from the bridge it was seen to have sustained a direct hit. The most difficult target attempted that night had been destroyed — an indication of the flying skills of the pilot who was to become one of the most famous flyers of World War II.

Sergeant Harpham was unable to establish his position in the poor visibility as the weather worsened. After stooging around in the overcast for some time, he turned L4057 for home, retaining his bombs.

Likewise, crew members of L4055 were unable to identify a worthwhile target

Aircraftman William Thornton, wireless operator

Sergeant Peter Josse, navigator

and Sergeant Jenkins set course out over the North Sea. They too were bringing their bomb-load home — bombs which would end up on a hillside at Holme, a small village near Holmfirth.

For the seven Hampdens approaching England, each crossing the English coastline at varying times after 2 am, a large weather front awaited them. Stan Harpham recalls the stress of that night as he sought to bring his aircraft safely down.

"We received a diversion to another field, but our 'Syko' code machine could only make out '. . . hall'. I assumed from this that we were to locate Stradishall; however, I was lucky enough to catch a glimpse of a beacon through the cloud and identified Mildenhall. After a desperate circuit or two the full aerodrome lights were put on and I somehow got in."

For Sergeant Jenkins in L4055 there was no chance sighting of an aerodrome beacon. He flew on unaware of the diversion to the airfields of Norfolk where his fellow pilots were putting down.

Fifty miles from the coast they had been challenged over the radio by one of the MF/DF stations and had responded with the correct identification signal. But after that, nothing was heard on the frequencies used to home in on the airfields.

During the last fifty miles the wireless must have given out. Without navigation aids and in bad weather Sergeant Josse, who was navigating, would have been unable to assist Sergeant Jenkins to find an airfield.

After flying for some time above cloud with fuel getting low, Jenkins would have had to consider his alternatives; either risk dropping through the cloud cover and attempting a landing where he could, or baling out. He opted for descent through cloud — in those days crews valued their charges highly, and

Inside an Hampden looking towards the pilot's position. Photograph taken from the lower rear gunner's position. Note the Elsan lavatory placed directly behind the pilot's cockpit; also the alloy ladder stowed at the side for entry and exit over the port wing root.

'she' had to be saved if at all possible.

An explosion awoke ARP Warden Mrs Doris Haigh at around 4 am. She dressed in a hurry and scrambled up the hillside to where she could see flames and smoke belching up from the corner of a field, on the side of Holme Moss. Her attempts to reach the blazing wreckage were thwarted as exploding ammunition hosed the area. She crouched behind a dry-stone wall to shelter from the spraying bullets. It was getting light before she could get anywhere near the wreckage — it was then that she could see that her efforts were in vain. The four crewmen had been killed upon impact with the ground.

A week later, children playing near the wreckage found an unexploded bomb, which was later detonated at the crash site by Royal Engineers of the 35th Bomb Disposal Section. The wreckage of L4055 remained on the site throughout the summer, and was finally removed in the winter of the same year. An eight-man salvage team dismantled the larger portions of twisted metal and the pieces were dragged down to a Queen Mary trailer.

At the crash site today there is a slight crater with a stream running through it and a partially demolished dry-stone wall, which L4055 ploughed through over fifty years ago.

The pilot, Sergeant Jenkins, and navigator, Peter Josse, were buried together with full military honours in the old churchyard at Nettleham, Lincolnshire.

Three days after the raid on the rail network, the British Army was lifted from the Dunkirk beaches. Bomber Command's contribution to delaying the German advance could only have been of irritation value. In those days bomb-loads were insignificant, navigational aids barely adequate and bomb-laying techniques hardly developed — and the crews (by their own admission) novices, for the most part.

With the wireless inoperative and in tenth-tenth's cloud cover, the crew of L4055 stood little chance once the decision had been made to stay with the aircraft, and opt for descent in the region of the Pennine mountain range.

The crash site as it is today; in the foreground is the crater caused when one of the bombs was exploded by a bomb-disposal squad of the Royal Engineers.

Defiant N1766, 96 Squadron, RAF, flying from Cranage to Digby and return on night-flying practice and air tests, crashed Rowlee Pasture, 12th April, 1941.

Map reference 154905 ● Map key number 27

The sole passenger aboard the twin-engined Oxford was a black Labrador by the name of 'Skeeta'. Flight-Lieutenant Walter Matthews, a New Zealander, was delivering him to the commanding officer of 116 Squadron.

Skeeta's first master, another New Zealand pilot by the name of Paul Rabone, had been posted as missing on 24th July, 1944, whilst engaged in a daylight 'Ranger' mission over Germany, flying a Mosquito. The dog was being delivered to his new master.

Rabone had been in the process of building a reputation for himself as a fighter pilot at the time that he went missing — his combat life up until that time had been most eventful. He was among the few RAF personnel who had arrived in France the day before war was declared on Germany on September 3rd, 1939. By April 1941 he had baled out six times. The last time he jumped was over Derbyshire — the wreckage of that machine lies around a crater on Rowlee Pasture, above Derwent Reservoir.

Rabone was first shot down during a bombing raid on the German-held bridge at Maastricht in Holland. Those early missions carried out by British bomber squadrons, in an attempt to slow down the mighty German Blitzkrieg machine, were pitiful. Outdated and obsolescent Fairey Battles struggled through skies filled with flak thrown up by mobile anti-aircraft units, to drop their inadequate bomb-loads around the bridge.

Rabone's Battle sustained severe flak damage and he, with his other two crew members, was forced to bale out. The three of them landed safely, but found themselves behind German lines.

The roads in Belgium, where they had dropped, were thronged with refugees fleeing they knew not where; Rabone and his crew disguised themselves in civilian clothes, mingled with the crowds on the dusty roads and succeeded in passing unnoticed by the German soldiers.

Upon reaching a grass landing-strip at Dieppe he discovered three disabled Hurricane fighters that the ground crews were about to destroy, to save them falling into the hands of the advancing enemy. Using parts from two of them he succeeded in making the third flyable and took off for England and safety. After a short rest he was back with his squadron and operating over France — only to be shot down for the second time.

On that occasion a Messerschmitt 109 caught him whilst he was on a bombing raid to destroy a bridge over the Seine. The Fairey Battle's defensive armament — a single forward-firing machine-gun and a single machine-gun manned by the wireless operator — was no deterrent to

Flight Lieutenant Paul Rabone with his dog 'Skeeta'.

the attacking fighter, and yet again Rabone and his crew had to abandon their aircraft. On that occasion they did land behind their own lines, and four days later they were back in England with 88 Squadron.

In August 1940 he was posted to a fighter squadron and after some intensive training on Hurricanes at Drem, in Scotland, Rabone was ready to give out some punishment to the enemy, rather than being always on the receiving end.

His opportunity came in October when he was posted to Tangmere, near the south coast. Although the Battle of Britain had been fought and won, there was still plenty of activity over the English Channel, as Rabone discovered on his first patrol. 20,000 feet over Portsmouth he was attacked by fifty plus Me 109s — but managed to evade their fire and escaped damage.

The following day Rabone was patrolling at 27,000 feet along with fighters from five other squadrons. The fighter wing met a formation of Me 109s and battle commenced. Rabone tagged onto a German fighter and shot it up. As he watched it spin away earthwards, pouring black smoke, he felt his Hurricane shudder as bullets thumped into the fuselage and wings. The fighter stopped responding to the controls and for the third time had to take his leave. He made a safe landing at Dungeness, if a little too close to the sea for comfort.

Next day, Rabone bagged his second victim, another Me 109 — again he was raked with bullets but he managed to struggle home. Upon landing he and his rigger counted thirty-two holes in his aircraft.

The month of November, and another German fighter fell victim to Rabone's guns — but now the young pilot was to move on to another phase in his fighting career, night fighting.

Luftwaffe tactics had undergone a change — the bombers came over by night

Boulton Paul's appealing publicity picture of the Defiant showing its clean, attractive lines.

to attack the cities, causing the defences to address the problems of location and interception at night. It was during that period in November that Rabone had to jump twice to save his life, although on those occasions this wasn't brought about through enemy action.

A severe storm at 22,000 feet caused him to make his first jump at night — he landed safely near Selsey Bill. Again at night, on patrol high over the City of London, his engine suddenly packed in and refused to re-start. Over the side again for the fifth time and, on this occasion, over a built-up area. Where would he land — there was a real prospect of broken bones? Rabone floated down and landed neatly in Green Park.

During December, whilst with 96 Squadron, Rabone was given a Night Visual Capacity Test . . . And the result? Exceptional! The squadron moved up north for the night defence of Liverpool and district.

It was at Cranage that Paul Rabone was introduced to the Boulton & Paul Defiant — it was not to be a happy association, and would end in his sixth jump,

the aircraft's remains left decorating a hill in the Peak District National Park, Derbyshire.

Introduced into Fighter Command in May 1940, the Defiant proved to be a failure. All the armaments of the two-seater fighter were concentrated in a single turret situated behind the pilot. It was impossible for the gunner manning four machine-guns to anticipate his pilot's manoeuvres and take aim on a moving target. After heavy losses against the more conventional forward-firing fighters, the type was switched to a night-fighter role. Pilots of 96 Squadron were among the recipients of that dubious steed and, for the most part, didn't take to it. To them its shortcomings were obvious and consequently they hung onto their Hurricanes, and only reluctantly took the two-seater on patrol.

Paul Rabone was put in command of A Flight, which consisted of four aircraft, and was placed on detachment at Squires Gate. He firmly marked the occasion by taking up the well-tried and proven 'Hurrybird' and shooting down his first enemy bomber at night — and those were

Flying Officer Vesley

burst, which caused the bomber to catch fire as it dropped towards the sea off Blackpool.

In the months following, a number of mishaps with the newly acquired Defiants did not endear that particular type to the pilots of 96 Squadron. There was a full moon on 12th March and the weather was perfect for intercepting raiders, and more than the usual number of Defiants were airborne. Individual fighters were being vectored on to enemy raiders by ground control.

Over Liverpool Rabone had to turn for base, Defiant N1766 having suffered gun failure.

Another 96 Squadron Defiant crew actually spotted an enemy bomber and identified it as a Heinkel 111. The pilot, Flight-Sergeant Taylor, lined the German bomber up for his gunner, but when Flight-Sergeant Broughton tried to fire, the guns jammed. The enemy bomber dived away steeply, putting up defensive fire – as it happened, no bullets made contact with the Defiant. Another Defiant which experienced similiar problems that night, did not get off so lightly, however.

Defiant N1803, piloted by a Czechoslovakian, Flying-Officer Vesley, was able to intercept another Heinkel 111. His air-gunner, Flight-Sergeant Haycock, filled his sights with the black silhouette and operated the trigger – nothing! The multiple Vickers machineguns failed to fire. Vesley formated on the bomber, expecting his gunner to clear the trouble. Even when the German pilot took evasive action, Vesley followed and determinedly flew alongside. During all that time Haycock worked frantically on the four machine-guns. Eventually, a machine-gun aboard the Heinkel was brought to bear on the persistent Defiant and Vesley was wounded in the head, chest, shoulder and left arm, and immediately losing consciousness. When he came round, he found the Defiant in a

the days before air-to-air radar – bringing his personal total to four enemy aircraft destroyed in combat.

Flying-Officer Rabone had been ordered to patrol Formby at 14,000 feet; because of heavy cloud obscuring the ground he was out of position when suddenly he sighted the glow from the exhausts of a twin-engined bomber, slightly above him and about 50 yards ahead. Bringing the nose of his Hurricane up slightly he opened fire into the belly of the aircraft, which promptly went into a dive. He followed and got in another

spin and with some difficulty regained control. The badly injured pilot courageously brought his plane home and put it down safely.

That same night Flight-Sergeant McNare intercepted another Heinkel and shot it down near Widnes – he was flying a Hurricane.

More frustration was to follow for the crews flying the Defiants. On the night of 10th April, 1941, the expected Luftwaffe aerial attack on Birmingham materialised. The night-fighter defences were ready – anticipating the enemy attack 96 Squadron joined up with 256 (Defiant) Squadron at Ternhill, which was twenty-five miles nearer the target city.

From the outset things began to go wrong for the Defiant crews of 96 Squadron. Out of the eight aircraft from that squadron involved, only two managed to keep up a sustained patrol over the blitzed city – not one of the German raiders was sighted. The usual crop of failures and breakdowns dogged the Defiant crews, thus causing the majority of aircraft to become unserviceable.

Rabone's Defiant N3438 developed trouble 10,000 feet over the target city when its hydraulic pump burst.

Truly a disappointing show as far as the pilots were concerned – they seemed helpless to prevent the Luftwaffe from devastating the cities assigned to their protection. When they had operated with Hurricanes they had achieved some results, but since going over to their failure-prone Defiants, everything had gone wrong. Morale was at a low ebb for 96 Squadron by April 1941. Two days after the abortive attempt to intercept the German night-bombers – 12th April – Rabone baled out for the sixth and last time.

Little flying was being done, certainly none at night, when Rabone took off in Defiant N1766, the very same aircraft that had let him and his air-gunner,

Flying Officer John Ritchie (later squadron leader)

Sergeant Irvine, down the previous month when the guns had jammed over Liverpool. On this occasion the crewman in the gun turret was Flying Officer Ritchie. It was a routine trip, a night-flying exercise from Cranage to Digby in Lincolnshire and return.

It was twenty past nine on a black, cloudy night and they were twenty miles off track over the desolate Dark Peak area. At around 3,000 feet the two of them abandoned the machine, which promptly thudded into Rowlee Pasture. Both men landed safely, although Ritchie was cross-examined by a suspicious farmer who mistook him for a German flier. Through his Scottish accent Ritchie assured the puzzled local that he was truly British.

Over 40 years after the event John Ritchie explained what took place on that night:

"We took off on a normal training flight and all went well on the outward journey. Coming back we were flying below cloud, but as the weather worsened Paul decided to climb above cloud, in view of the high

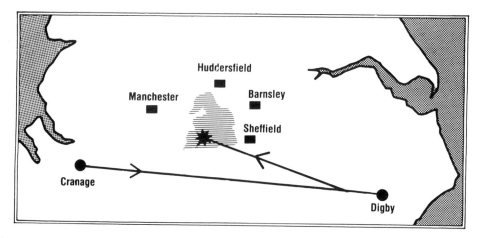

ground that we had to cross. At some point he called up and asked for a vector to base, to which he received a jumbled reply. Several more calls for assistance were put out but the replies were indecipherable. Shortly after that the radio transmitter packed up completely, and Paul informed me that he was not particularly happy about the engine.

"We discussed the situation and having no R/T, and not knowing where we were, we decided to abandon the aircraft having gained a little more height.

"After having left the aircraft and

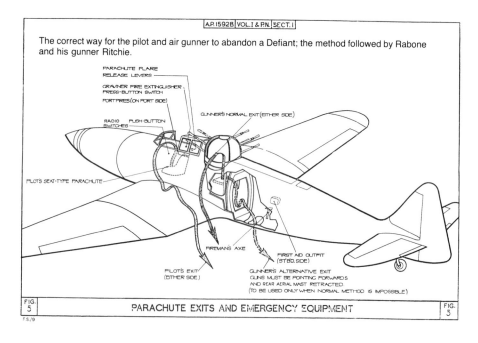

A.P.1592B VOL. I & P.N. SECT. I

The correct way for the pilot and air gunner to abandon a Defiant; the method followed by Rabone and his gunner Ritchie.

PARACHUTE FLARE RELEASE LEVERS

GRAVINER FIRE EXTINGUISHER PRESS-BUTTON SWITCH

PORTFIRES (ON PORT SIDE)

RADIO PUSH-BUTTON SWITCHES

GUNNER'S NORMAL EXIT (EITHER SIDE)

PILOTS SEAT-TYPE PARACHUTE

FIREMAN'S AXE

FIRST AID OUTFIT (STBD. SIDE)

PILOT'S EXIT (EITHER SIDE)

GUNNER'S ALTERNATIVE EXIT GUNS MUST BE POINTING FORWARDS AND REAR AERIAL MAST RETRACTED. (TO BE USED ONLY WHEN NORMAL METHOD IS IMPOSSIBLE)

FIG. 5

PARACHUTE EXITS AND EMERGENCY EQUIPMENT

FIG. 5

F.5./9

floating down, I could see water – and hoped that I wouldn't land in that! Fortunately, the ground seemed to rush up and hit me. I gathered up my parachute and set off down the hill – but some way down decided the 'chute was a nuisance so I discarded it. I eventually came to a road and tossed a coin to see in which direction I should go. I didn't have too far to walk before I saw the light of a farmhouse. I knocked on the door and was met by a farmer brandishing a shotgun. There was a telephone at the farm and I asked him to call the police, who arrived eventually and assured me that Paul had been picked up. One little courtesy was afforded me by the police. They stopped at a pub, knocked the landlord up and got me a very large whisky – which I certainly needed!

"After debriefing at the Squadron we were sent smartly back into the air once again . . ."

Twenty days later Rabone was posted out to 85 Squadron as 'Supernumerary for Flying' – a pilot extra to complement. At least his new squadron was equipped with the Douglas Havoc as a night-fighter – not the dreaded Defiant.

In June 1943 Rabone joined 23 Squadron in the Mediterranean theatre and teamed up with navigator Pilot-Officer Johns. They were engaged in intruder missions over Sicily and Italy, flying Mosquitoes. This duo shot up trains, bombed railways, destroyed vehicle columns, and on one occasion caught three seaplanes sitting on the water, wrecking them. The Mosquito was the perfect steed for him.

During that period Rabone brought down three more German bombers. As an intruder pilot he was rated 'excellent'.

In November 1943 he returned to England and seven months later the Allies invaded Europe; Rabone was posted to 515 Squadron, which until that time had only operated at night; now they were about to switch to daylight Ranger raids

FROM A PAINTING BY RONI
Flight Lieutenant Paul Rabone

over Europe. An experienced day-ranger pilot was needed to show the other pilots the ropes.

On 21st June, Rabone caught an Me110 which was just taking off and shot it down in flames – 515's first daylight victory. By the end of the month the squadron's pilots were claiming five German aircraft brought down – three of them were Rabone's, bringing his personal score of enemy aircraft destroyed to ten.

The following month he was posted back to 23 Squadron and on 24th July, 1944, after twelve days' leave, Paul Rabone and Flying-Officer Johns took off on another day-ranger operation. They failed to return from that mission and no trace was ever found of them.

Rabone's dog, Skeeta, was passed on to his new master, and back in New Zealand his wife Pamela eventually remarried.

On a hillside in Derbyshire lies the scattered remains of a Defiant – an unworthy mount for an ace, but the only remaining memorial to the young New Zealand pilot, Paul Rabone.

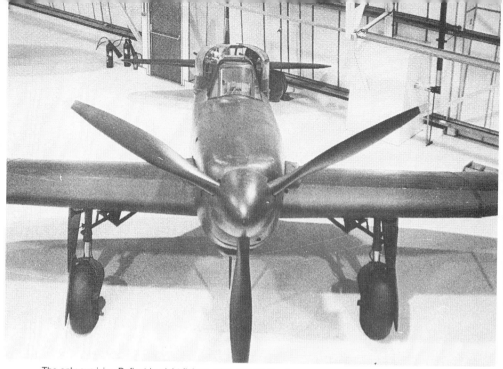

The only surviving Defiant in night-fighter guise at RAF Hendon.

Crash site on Rowlee Pasture featuring a fair size crater and metal fragments. *MIKE LAWSON*

In August 1980 a team of local enthusiasts using vintage military vehicles undertook the task of reclaiming the Defiant's Rolls Royce engine.

Author cleaning up the Defiant's Rolls Royce engine for display at the Air and Space Museum, Manchester.

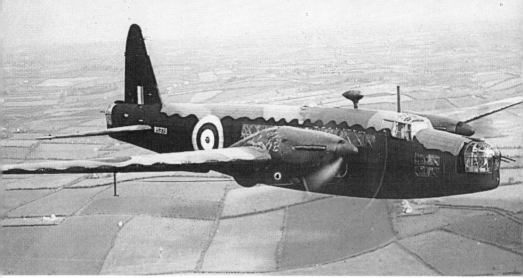

Wellington W5719, 150 Squadron, RAF, returning to base at Snaith from a bombing raid on Cologne, crashed at Upper Tor, 31st July, 1941.

Map reference 111877 ● Map key number 28

In the early months of World War II both the Luftwaffe and RAF Bomber Command exercised restraint in the use of their bomber aircraft. Each side wished to avoid reprisals by accidentally killing civilians in bombing raids; consequently, targets consisted mainly of the opposing nations' warships, plus harmless leaflet-dropping excursions by the RAF at night over Germany.

However, with the German invasion of the Low Countries in May 1940, the 'kid gloves' came off and concern for civilian life and property was abandoned. This took a particularly nasty turn for the worse as the Luftwaffe and Bomber Command each discovered that their attempts to destroy military targets, such as munition factories, port installations, and so on, were ineffective. The cities of the enemy were easier to locate, so both sides began a policy of deliberately attacking the civilian population.

There followed a period of retaliation raids; for example, the Luftwaffe attacked Coventry and Southampton, so the RAF bombed Mannheim; Berlin was also attacked, which in turn provoked raids on London. Demoralisation of the enemy by submitting the people to sustained bombardment from the air was the line of justification taken by the leaders. But, rather than destroying the people's will to fight on, the bombing of civilians served instead to strengthen their resolve to 'see it through together'.

As a policy, strategic bombing of cities it failed to achieve the desired results, but nevertheless, it was to continue until the war ended — and many cities had been reduced to rubble.

For the RAF bomber crews who had to carry out the orders of the policy-makers, locating a German city at night and unloading explosives on it often proved a difficult task in the days before effective navigational aids.

Daylight excursions over enemy territory by bombers had been abandoned, for the most part, by Bomber Command — it had proved too costly in men and machines. Consequently, twin-engined Hamp-

27

Squadron photograph showing Sergeant Parrot, pilot of W5719; next to him is Sergeant Webber, wireless operator and on the end Sergeant Monk, air gunner.

A. WELDON

dens, Whitleys and Wellingtons, with meagre bomb-loads, took off most nights of the week, frequently in unfavourable weather conditions, for a German city. The return trip could be around 800 miles and take up to six hours. During all that time crews endured cramped, cold and draughty conditions, fired at by anti-aircraft defences and night-fighters, whilst seeking to find their way at night, sometimes in atrocious weather.

It was during this period of pioneer bombing of German cities that a Wellington, returning with its bomb-load, hit a hillside in Edale, exploding and flinging clear the rear gun-turret and its occupant.

It was July 1941 and 150 Squadron had just recently moved from Newton in Nottinghamshire to Snaith in Yorkshire. It had been a bad period for the squadron – they had suffered heavy losses during the month, and at one time only two aircraft remained from a full complement of twelve and two in reserve.

Among the replacements for 150 Squadron at Snaith was Sergeant Earl Tilley, who was to experience an amazing escape on the last day of July.

Earl Tilley joined the crew of 'S' for Sugar as rear gunner – in most instances the most dangerous crew position in a British bomber. German night-fighters would invariably concentrate their initial attack on that position. If 'Tail-End Charlie' could be put out of action, then usually the fate of the aircraft was sealed.

Through the official pipeline came the order for another raid for 150 Squadron. Executive Orders for Operation No. 6, the bombing of Cologne, on the Rhine, involved the use of eight aircraft for the night of 30th July, 1941. Weather conditions throughout the day were bad – low cloud covered the airfield and heavy rain drenched the runways. It looked to the waiting crews as though there might be a cancellation; they could well spend the night in their beds rather than at 15,000

Sergeant Earl Tilley, rear gunner

feet over the North Sea and Germany. The eight Wellingtons had been attended by the ground crews and were each loaded with a 1,000-pound bomb and four 500-pounders. The aircraft stood in the pouring rain, awaiting the men who would take them up.

At 10.30 in the evening the rain abated and the word came through to go. Once the crews had climbed aboard they went through the series of checks – and even then the raid might have been cancelled, but the rain held off and at 11.20 pm the first bomber had taxied into position for take-off.

It was 'S' for Sugar that was to be the first one off the ground, piloted by Sergeant 'Tiny' Parrott; second pilot was Sergeant Haswell. Navigating the 450

Tail-end of a Wellington; the complete turret of W5719 was flung off, with Earl Tilley inside, when the bomber struck Upper Tor.

miles to Cologne and back was Sergeant Evelle, a Canadian; wireless operator was Sergeant Webber. And protecting Wellington W5719, crouched up in the nose turret, was Sergeant Denis Monk from Stockport. Taking care of possible stern attacks was another Canadian, Sergeant Earl Tilley − 'Tail-End Charlie'.

There was to be no cancellation and at 11.25 pm 'S' for Sugar was climbing into the black overcast, followed twenty minutes later by a second Wellington − with the rest following at five-minute intervals. By ten past one the squadron had been swallowed up and forty-eight

men were en route for Germany − five of them would not be coming back, and one would not be returning to Snaith for six months.

From his isolated position in the tail gun-turret, Earl Tilley observed the events of that tragic flight.

"We ran into heavy cloud over the North Sea − and after we crossed the enemy coast, we flew into a bad electrical storm, with thunder and lightning all around us. We tried to climb over the storm and then to go round it, but with no success. Our Skipper decided to return to base with our bomb-load. When we reached the English coast the cloud cover

Crash site, clearly showing the rock-strewn slope down which the rear turret bounced with Earl Tilley inside on the night of 31st July, 1941.

had moved inland. To make matters worse our radio had been rendered U/S by the electrical storm.

"Our navigator had figured that we had crossed the coast in the vicinity of the Wash. All of us were looking for an opening in the cloud, trying to see something that we could identify, so as to establish our position.

"Our Skipper must have dropped through the clouds when he estimated that we should have been over our base.

The next thing that I remember, I was lying on the ground and the aircraft was burning. I tried to get away from the crash as I remembered that we still had the bombs on board. I had great difficulty in trying to walk — I crawled and then rolled away before losing consciousness.

"The next thing that I recall was hearing voices and it was daylight. I was taken to a house in a nearby village, and from there to a hospital in Manchester."

Six months later Earl Tilley returned to 150 Squadron at Snaith, only to be shot down over Holland in June 1942, and taken prisoner.

Wellington W5719 had struck Edale Moor at Upper Tor. The impact and resulting explosion had blown clear the rear turret and its occupant, Sergeant Tilley.

Of the other seven aircraft that had set out to bomb the citizens of Cologne, five found their target and bombed a large fire that they found burning there. The heavy cloud stretched over the city and they were unable to see any results from their bombing. Two other Wellingtons bombed alternative targets in Belgium.

Manning the rear gun-turret of a British bomber over Germany may have proved to be the most dangerous crew position; but should a flying accident occur, then there could be definite advantages in being 'Tail-End Charlie'.

Some scraps remain on the hillside today.

Lysander V9403, 6 Anti-Aircraft Co-operation Unit, flying from Ringway to Rhyl for training duties, turned on a wrong heading and crashed on Slate Pit Moss, 19th August, 1941.

Map reference 041033 ● Map key number 29

In the early hours of 19th August, 1941, a Lysander of 6 Anti-Aircraft Co-operation Unit crashed on the moors above Chew Valley, trapping the pilot and wireless operator in the wreckage. For two days the injured men lay awaiting rescue, and the pilot watched helplessly as an air search was concentrated on an area of moorland just three miles away, where a Swordfish of the Fleet Air Arm had crashed the previous year. The following is Pilot Officer Hoddinott's own account of the accident.

"My story begins on August 18th, 1941, at which time I was a pilot-officer in the Royal Air Force. The unit in which I was serving at that time was an Anti-Aircraft Co-operation Unit, stationed at Ringway Airport, Manchester. One of our duties

was to provide aircraft by day and night for the training of anti-aircraft guns and searchlight units.

"I think that it is true to say that I was one of the more experienced members of our unit, having completed more than one thousand hours' flying as a pilot on some sixteen different types of single— and twin-engined aircraft.

"On the night of 18th/19th August, I was detailed to fly a Lysander aircraft to the Rhyl area for two hours' co-operation with guns and searchlights there.

"In those comparatively early days of the war, being classed as a non-operational unit, our aircraft, though armed, were not equipped with radio telephony. The only navigational aid we possessed was wireless telegraphy,

Aircraftman Fred Hoddinott

checks, and also set my gyro-compass by reference to the magnetic compass.

"For the benefit of the lay-reader, I should explain that the gyro-compass is a calibrated card mounted on a gyroscope, and uses the gyroscopic principle of rigidity. It is therefore a much more stable directional reference than the magnetic compass, which is north-seeking and affected by acceleration, deceleration and turning. Due to the rotation of the earth, however, precession takes place, and it is necessary to reset the gyro-indicator by reference to the magnetic compass at frequent intervals during the flight.

"I then proceeded to take off into the wind along the line of five small, battery operated glim lamps. These were invisible from the air above a height of about 1,000 feet.

"At 500 feet and still climbing I circled the airfield, and set course for Chester so as to avoid the balloon barrage at Liverpool. We flew into the cloud at less than 2,000 feet, but that did not worry me in view of the met. forecast of only five-tenths cloud.

"Over the intercom I could hear my wireless operator trying to contact the ground station, to obtain the usual bearing and thus confirm that we were following the correct course. Everything appeared to be just another routine flight.

"We had been flying for about fifteen minutes without a sign of a break in the cloud, and I decided that it was time to check the directional gyro-indicator with the magnetic compass. I was suprised to find that there was a difference of about 160 degrees between the two instruments, and instead of flying on a south-westerly course, I was in fact on a north north-easterly heading.

"I decided that the directional gyro was faulty, and instead of flying on a straight course, I had been following the directional gyro in a very gradual turn to starboard. If my deductions were correct,

through the medium of a wireless operator. Consequently, night sorties could only be carried out in reasonable flying conditions.

"I arrived at the airfield in ample time for a 2.30am take-off and studied the weather forecast for the area, provided by the Meteorological Office. This reported five-tenths cloud at 2,000 feet; in other words half the sky would be covered in clouds, with the cloud base at 2,000 above sea level. Not a particularly good forecast for the job that I had to do, but worth trying. I advised my wireless operator, and the duty pilot in the control tower, that I would be taking off as planned.

"Together with my wireless operator I proceeded to the aircraft where I started up the engine and carried out the usual pre-flight cockpit drill and engine tests; then I taxied out to the take-off position. At that point I carried out the usual

we could be dangerously close to the balloon barrage over Liverpool. I was still flying in cloud at a height of 2,500 feet — not a very healthy position to be in. Therefore, I immediately turned onto a southerly course on the magnetic compass, and decided to reduce height in order to break clear of the cloud. My estimation of our position at that time was that we were to the north of Chester, a low lying area where I could safely reduce height to 1,000 feet.

"Even in the blackout, and on the darkest of nights, one could alsways pick out the railway marshalling yards at Chester, and also the outline of the Dee estuary. I reduced speed and commenced a gradual descent.

"At 2,000 feet we were still in cloud, then with the altimeter registering just over 1,900 feet, the dark grey of the cloud suddenly changed to pitch black — we had struck the ground.

"I must have been knocked unconscious as the next recollection I had was,

that I was in a half-sitting, half-reclining position in the remains of the wrecked aircraft. The windscreen, instrument panel, cockpit and engine cowling had all disappeared. What remained of the engine was a mess of twisted metal forced back against my legs. There was a strong smell of burning oil.

"My thoughts immediately went to the petrol tank, situated just behind me, which must have been three-parts full when we crashed. I wondered if the whole lot would go up in flames. I was unable to turn around, but called out to my wireless operator. His reply cut me to the quick: 'I thought that you were supposed to be a good pilot!' I was later to learn that his parting words to his wife the evening before were that she had nothing to worry about because he was flying with me that night. He too was trapped by his legs, although not badly injured.

"I tried to pull my legs free, but only succeeded in pulling my left leg out of my flying-boot, leaving the boot firmly

Flying Officer Fred Hoddinott (centre) at Ringway, Manchester.

wedged in the wreckage of the engine. Once the danger of fire had passed I was not unduly worried, as I was sure that with the arrival of daylight we would very soon be found. I was not in any pain; perhaps that was due to the shock and the severity of my injuries.

"I remember seeing what appeared to be a lake a short distance ahead, but with the arrival of daylight it turned out to be a piece of engine cowling just a few feet ahead of the wreckage.

"Another surprise awaited with the arrival of dawn. I had expected to see fields, trees, hedges and possibly a farm house—instead there was nothing but barren moorland as far as the eye could see.

"From time to time I leaned forward and tried to move some of the engine wreckage so as to free my right leg, but I must have been very weak. Blood from a gash in my forehead ran freely whenever I exerted myself and so I was obliged to lie back again without having made any progress.

"As the day wore on, my wireless operator became very despondent, frequently praying and telling me that we would never be found. I could not see him, for he was trapped in the rear part of the fuselage, but I gathered from what he said that he could not see out. It must have been harder for him, at least I was out in the open air, and thus able to look for any sign of activity in the surrounding countryside. But there was no sign of activity on that moor. I had no idea of the time because my watch had been torn from my wrist upon impact with the ground, but I estimated that it must have been late afternoon when I saw an aircraft.

"It seemed to be circling an area in the distance and I recognised it as a type used by our unit—I was convinced that the crew were looking for us.

"The aircraft continued flying round an area some distance from us. Although I had Very light cartridges in the pocket of my flying suit, I could not use them without the pistol, which was lost in the wreckage as also was the torch which I invariably took with me at night. I told my wireless operator that the aircraft was obviously searching for us, and that it would not be long before we were found. However, we were to be disappointed, because it flew off in the opposite direction without having seen us. We were in for another night on the moor.

"I later learned that the aircraft was in fact from our unit and searching for us. The pilot had spotted wreckage and directed a search party to the spot, only to find that it was the remains of another aircraft from a fatal crash the previous year [see Book One, log 13].

"During that night we heard air-raid sirens sounding which raised our hopes of rescue, because we felt that the Home Guard and Wardens would be out and about, but what we did not appreciate at the time was that we were down in an uninhabited area.

"With the arrival of dawn my foremost preoccupation was with a raging thirst. It began to rain a little and I held my head back to catch the drops, but failed. The day wore on without further incident, and just as light seemed to be fading, a figure appeared, running and stumbling over the rough moorland.

"I told my wireless operator that rescue was on the way, whereupon he began shouting, urging the man to hurry, and continued to do so until our rescuer stood over us.

"I was desperately thirsty and asked the man to remove the batteries from my torch case and use it to get me a drink of water from one of the puddles that were spread about. I remember that he objected, pointing out that the peat water was unfit to drink. My insistence won out and I had the most refreshing drink of my life.

"Here I should say that although I had

previously thought that night was falling, it really was still the middle of the day—probably I was drifting towards death's door.

"My recollections of events from that point on are very hazy. I remember the man leaving and returning some time later with several others. It only took two of them to remove the engine from my leg, with what appeared to be the greatest of ease, and I was lifted free and laid on a stretcher. It seemed that I was carried for a considerable distance, crossing at least one stream. I recall feeling the water on my back when one of the stretcher-bearers lost his footing. When we arrived at the waiting ambulance I was given a drink of hot, sweet tea from a saucer. It was delicious and I would have liked more, but the ambulance men were anxious to get moving.

"The next thing that I remember was lying in a hospital bed, under a framework of electric lamps. The first few days in hospital at Ashton-under-Lyne must have been a series of periods of consciousness and unconsciousness, but due to the untiring efforts of the surgeons, and the constant devotion of the nursing staff, I was soon well on the road to recovery.

"The history of my recovery is another story, however; let it suffice to say that after sixteen weeks I was well enough to be moved to a Royal Air Force hospital. After a further nine weeks I was fit enough to return to my unit where there followed three months of non-flying duties. I was then passed fit for flying duties, and completed a further nine hundred hours flying as pilot and captain of aircraft before the war ended.

"My wireless operator was not so fortunate, for he died a few days after our admission to hospital, although I was not allowed to discover that fact until some months afterwards. Although he did not have injuries as serious as I had, the nature of the damage to his limbs was

Mr Hoddinott visited the site exactly to the day forty years later.

more than likely a contributory factor to his death.

"Bearing this out is the letter that the surgeon wrote to me after my recovery: *There has been a good deal of discussion lately in the medical press with regard to deaths resulting from 'crush injuries'—the point being that when a limb is compressed and its blood supply is interfered with the limb swells up, but upon the removal of the obstruction, the kidneys get damaged and death results from this cause. In your case your wounds were left open for many days and I am inclined to think that the poisons accumulated in your limb worked out of your open wounds, and so your kidneys and life were saved.*

"It was not until I was well on the way to recovery that I was able to reason out exactly what happened leading up to the crash. Until that time I had been convinced that the altimeter had been faulty, but then I asked my wife to bring me a map so that I could see where the hospital was, and so the approximate position of the crash. It was only then that I realised that there nothing wrong with the altimeter; we had in fact crashed on the top of the Pennines, where they reach a height of almost two thousand feet above sea level.

"It was in fact the directional gyro that was faulty and instead of flying on a west- south-westerly course, I had in fact flown on a north-easterly course and thus in the opposite direction.

"Unlike 'Wrong Way' Corrigan—who achieved fame by taking off from an airfield on the east coast of America with the intention of flying inland, and instead landed in Ireland having flown the Atlantic by mistake—I almost achieved oblivion."

A recent picture of the crash site with only a few scraps of wood and metal to mark the spot.   *MIKE LAWTON*

KLIMCZAK

Wellington DV810, 21 Operational Training Unit, on a night exercise from Edge Hill, got lost in bad weather and crashed on Broomhead Moor, 9th December, 1942.

Private land ● Map key number 30

It was the foulest weather he had yet experienced while airborne. Nothing in his previous tour of operations with 214 Squadron on bombing sorties to Europe had prepared him for this. 'Tubby' Baker was annoyed at the situation he had been forced into by the powers that be.

Right up to take-off he had questioned the advisability of going. His insistence had caused the Officer Commanding Flying at Edge Hill to check with his superiors at Wing HQ — all to no avail; the instructions were to go. So there he was, flying at around 4,000 feet and approaching the east coast on a night cross-country trip in Wellington DV810; he was in the midst of thick cloud, buffeted by high winds and with a trainee crew.

From the time they had climbed into the black overcast at Edge Hill, which was a satellite of 21 Operational Training Unit at Moreton-in-Marsh, they were on 'dead reckoning'. Already they had discovered that the forecast winds amounted to something akin to a fairy story. The reality was pushing them about all over the inky-black sky — yes, Flying Officer Baker was definitely annoyed!

New aircrews were needed all the time and demands placed upon OTUs to turn out crews were pressing. The OCs Flying were being pushed to produce crews, not only to replace those lost through enemy action over Germany, and for the formation of new squadrons, but also for Coastal Command, the Middle East and the Far East. OTU training came at the end of a long period of instruction for each individual, and was where they were formed into crews and readied to

39

Wing Commander 'Tubby' Baker

take their place in one of the squadrons in Bomber Command. It was a five-month course involving eighty hours' flying time.

The training of a crew cost a staggering £10,000. Actual training was undertaken by instructors, who themselves were front-line crew members 'resting' between operations. There was, however, a continual shortage of men with operational experience who could serve as instructors, especially pilots. Consequently, those who proved suitable as instructors had to work overtime during their rest periods between operations. The risks were high as they were expected to operate in dangerous flying conditions in order to process crews through the system.

Conditions experienced by the trainee crews and their instructors of the six Wellingtons that took off on the night of 9th December, 1942, were far beyond what could be termed as reasonable.

That was Tubby Baker's considered opinion as the poor trainee navigator suggested that they must have reached their turning point, and gave a course change to take them back home to base. He accepted the navigator's judgement — after all, with all that muck swirling around them and high winds flinging them about like a cork on the ocean, the young lad's guess as to their position was as good as anyone's.

The pilot under training was Sergeant Turner. He dutifully turned onto the new heading. It was not a dual-control aircraft and Baker could only oversee the pupil's actions and make suggestions.

"We've got gas bags on the R/T, Skipper!" came the urgent call from Sergeant Morgan, who was the screen wireless operator (instructor).

Barrage balloons, defending industrial cities, had a small transmitter attached which emitted a warning signal so that Allied aircraft could avoid them. Wellington DV810 was flying blindly towards anti-aircraft balloons that could shatter a propeller or take a wing off. Turner was gripping the control column and peering ahead into the blackness, his nervousness apparent.

"I'd better take over, out you come." Baker motioned the pupil to leave the controls, signalling that he was taking control. Exchanging places in those circumstances was a risky business.

Once at the controls Baker checked their heading — westerly! The sound of the balloon squeakers was in no way diminishing, so he turned north to avoid being plucked from the sky — but the squeaks persisted. Taking the opposite direction, they encountered the squeaks again — and it soon became clear that they were stooging about over an industrial area.

They had to get below cloud and establish their position — they couldn't stay up there forever and there was no sign of the weather changing for the better. Coming down lower in their present position was out of the question. Balloons, factory chimneys, possible high ground, all ruled out that course of action. Baker announced his decision to the crew; he would head the aircraft to the east and once out over the North Sea, he would safely drop through the clouds, head back due west and pick up the coastline, where they could easily establish their position. Every one of the seven men on board — the two instructors and the five trainees — knew that they were in a dangerous situation. They were hopelessly lost.

After twenty minutes of flying due east, Baker decided that they must be somewhere out over the North Sea and proceeded to let down gently through the cloud.

"We came out at 1,200 feet and I saw, immediately below, what seemed to be another layer of cloud. I switched on the landing lamp, which in a Wellington was housed in the wing and shone straight down, until operated by a lever from the cockpit. Although that layer seemed a strange colour, it did look like cloud and I switched off the landing light.

" Almost immediately there was a bang and my port engine was on fire. I realised that what I took to be cloud was in fact the ground and I shouted to the crew to brace themselves for a crash. I throttled back both engines and began to hold off. Reaching up, I released my escape hatch and from the light of the blazing port engine, brought off a belly landing. I ordered the crew out and scrambled clear myself."

DV810 erupted into a mass of flames. Game birds evacuated the area in panic as light from the burning aircraft lit up the surrounding countryside and revealed large clumps of heather. They were on wild moorland, but where precisely?

Baker assembled the crew and ascertained that, apart from being shaken, everyone had got off without injury. He ordered them away from the bomber in case it exploded, which it duly did when they were a safe distance from it.

They decided not to wander off and risk becoming lost, but to stay where they were until daylight. There was the danger of walking off a cliff edge, considering their position close to the coast.

Baker was still annoyed. They could all have been killed. Had they been on an operational squadron the flight would have been cancelled because of the atrocious weather conditions — so why should they expect more from an inexperienced crew?

After about an hour sitting in the heather watching their aircraft being consumed by fire, they saw lights and heard voices approaching. Help was coming at last, possibly the inhabitants of a coastal village.

The crew was led off the moor and then transported to the nearby village of Stocksbridge — approximately seventy miles from the east coast. They had indeed been well and truly lost.

Whilst the members of the crew were taken to hospital suffering from mild shock and to have a check-up, Baker was put up at the local police sergeant's house. "I was treated very kindly indeed by the police sergeant's wife, and I was sorry that so much of my blood, from a gash on my head received in my hasty exit from the aircraft, was left on her pillows. For a long time afterwards the lady sent cakes to my unit, for which I was most greatful."

Upon returning to Edge Hill, Baker received a summons to report at once to the Officer Commanding Flying, HQ, Moreton- in-Marsh. The OC was in a black mood as Flying Officer Baker entered his office and saluted.

"Baker! What the bloody hell do you mean by crashing one of my aircraft?"

Baker was not a man to suffer fools gladly, and relaxing his at-attention stance, leaned forward, fixing his superior officer with a furious glare: "What the bloody hell do you mean by sending us up in such appalling weather?"

As far as Baker was concerned, there was nothing more to be said — the OC, eager to amass flying hours, had made a bad judgement. He turned and walked out of the office. They could take whatever action they liked against him — but to risk lives so unnecessarily seemed to be a far more serious crime than his insubordination.

It is significant that nothing was said further about what had taken place in the OC's office that day; or in fact, the wrecking of Wellington DV810.

Of the other five Wellingtons that had taken off on that stormy night, not one succeeded in returning to Edge Hill. One of the five crashed at Manston. Baker's skill in putting the bomber down in one piece, with only the light from the blazing

An Operational Training Unit preparing for a night exercise.

port engine to help him judge distance from the ground, thus saving himself and his crew, was indicative of what was to come. As was his handling of his superior officer.

By the time that the war had ended, Tubby Baker had reached the rank of wing-commander, and was commanding his own squadron. He had collected four decorations; the citation for his last, Bar to his Distinguished Service Order, read as follows:

Wing-Commander Baker has completed one hundred sorties, all of them were against strongly-defended enemy targets. He has displayed the highest qualities of skill and bravery throughout, his devotion to duty has been unfailing. Undeterred by the heaviest opposition, Wing-Commander Baker has pressed home his attacks with the greatest resolution. His achievements have won high praise.

An example of the type of operation that would have prompted the words 'pressing on against all odds' was seen in a sortie carried out on 27th March, 1943. Flying Officer Baker, as he was then, had learned of the formation of an elite bomber group that would lead and mark targets for the main bomber force, and he volunteered.

He was successful in his application, and joined the newly-formed Pathfinder Force when his posting came through to 7 Squadron operating from Oakington. They were equipped with Stirling four-engined bombers, and at the end of the month Baker's flying skills were put to the test.

Target for the night of the 27th was 'Big B' — Berlin. In the event the raid itself was not a success. For various reasons there were six early returns in 7 Squadron, and consequently there was a shortage of markers dropped on the target.

Baker, in Stirling R9255, reached the target and came in straight and level as

Tubby Baker celebrates the completion of a tour of operations with a welcome glass of bitter supplied by one of the groundcrew.

Tubby Baker (*third from right*) with his crew at Oakington while serving with 7 Squadron. The crewman third from left also appears on crew pictures in *Dark Peak Aircraft Wrecks book 1* on pages 116, 117 and 122.

a supporter, to bomb the indicators dropped by his fellow Pathfinders. They were coned by searchlights and began to sustain hits by flak. The port outer engine was peppered by shrapnel and suddenly stopped. Loss of power from the port inner compounded the problem, as Baker took evasive action to duck out of the blinding lights.

Having lost a great deal of height, and with reduced engine power making it impossible to regain it, Baker asked his navigator for a new route home — one that would avoid high ground and known defences. With two healthy engines roaring away on the starboard wing and nothing much doing in the way of power on the port side, the Stirling was difficult to control on that long homeward journey.

After five exhausting hours (making a total of eight and a quarter) nursing the struggling bomber, Oakington was reached. However, their trials were not quite over.

Baker selected 'undercarriage down' and three green lights lit up to indicate that all was well and that the wheels were locked in place. They were all set for landing — what they could not know was that the port-side tyre had been slashed with shrapnel.

The instant that the lumbering bomber touched the runway it slewed around and the tall, ungainly undercarriage was ripped away. The aircraft tore along through the field and came to a halt close to a cottage on the airfield perimeter. Six weary men climbed out shaken but unhurt.

Baker's skill and determination as a bomber pilot began to be recognised and in July 1944 he was given command of 635 Squadron. After D-Day he acted as Master Bomber on seventeen occasions.

On 18th July, 1944 the Second Army, under Montgomery, prepared to advance south of Caen. For three hours after dawn the heaviest concentrated air attack to date in support of ground forces took place. One of the targets was the village of Cagny, which housed concentrations of German infantry and anti-tank guns.

Tubby Baker receives the DFC from HRH King George VI.

The village was the target for the Pathfinder Force.

Piece of armour plating at crash site.

Master Bomber for Cagny was Tubby Baker. One hundred bombers were directed onto the target by the newly promoted Wing-Commander. After the attack a gigantic smoke pall hung suspended over the target like a shroud. The village of Cagny had been accurately marked and then obliterated.

When nations engage in acts of mass destruction against each other, inevitably, men with certain qualities appear. Out of necessity, leaders emerge from the masses of fighting men to take on responsibility. Master Bomber, Wing-Commander Stanley (Tubby) Baker, DSO and Bar, DFC and Bar, was such a man. Glimmers of his qualities as a pilot and leader could be seen in the happenings that took place on the night of 9th December, 1942, when he crash-landed a Wellington on Broomhead Moor, saving his own life and those of his trainee crew.

46

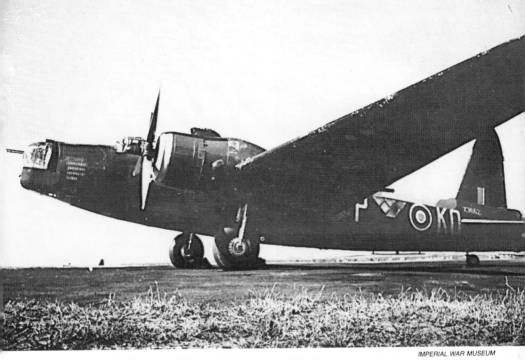

Wellington X3348, 427 Squadron, RCAF, returning to base at Croft from a bombing raid on Lorient, France, crashed on Blackden Edge, 26th January, 1943.

Map reference • Map key number 50

Towards the end of January 1943 the British Admiralty instigated an order to bomb two targets in occupied France. There was the likelihood of heavy loss of life among French civilians, but it was considered to be a regrettable but necessary expedient of war.

German U-boats, operating from French ports in the Bay of Biscay, were causing heavy losses among Allied convoys crossing the Atlantic. They had to be stopped, even if it meant sacrificing civilian lives. The Atlantic ports of St Nazaire and Lorient were the targets for the night of 25th January.

There was little hope of doing any real damage to the U-boats, for they sat in their lairs protected from air attack by many feet of reinforced concrete. At that period in the war the RAF did not possess a bomb that would penetrate the U-boat pens. The most that could be hoped for was the destruction of machinery shops and service facilities, in the surrounding dockyards.

For the crews of 427 (Lion) Squadron, RCAF, those days in January had presented them with frustrating raid cancellations, and days of no flying at all because of weather conditions. Out of four mine-laying sorties detailed for the squadron prior to the Lorient raid, three were cancelled at the last minute; a nerve-racking experience for the crews

47

Flight Lieutenant Carl Taylor, pilot

who sat tensed up in their individual aircraft awaiting the order to go.

Nine aircraft from 427 Squadron, 6 Group, were detailed for the raid on the afternoon of the 25th and stood bombed-up on the runway at Croft, County Durham.

For the men in "Z for Zebra" it was their fourth mission—they considered themselves veterans and keenly felt their battle experience in the presence of two newcomers to their crew. All six of them would undergo a new experience as that day ended; they would descend a hill that they had never gone up in the first place. Partly responsible for that experience was the navigator of X3348, 'Z for Zebra', Pilot Officer Martin. His story now follows:

"As one of the few men who enjoy the distinction of having walked down a mountain without first walking up it, I feel entitled to tell my story as to how it was done.

"In those days I was being paid to navigate an aircraft of the Royal Canadian Air Force, with an American Swede as pilot, a Batley, Yorkshire, man as bombardier, a Welshman as wireless operator/air-gunner, and a boy from Durham as rear-gunner. I originate from London.

"On that occasion we, being veterans of three operational flights, had a new pilot along to show him how things were done. It was to be an eye-opener for him!

"On 26th January, 1943, we all assembled at Wellington 'Z for Zebra'; we had a different wireless operator/air-gunner, as Taffy Baker, our regular man had a cold, and I am sure that he and the new pilot were suitably awed by our knowledgeable chatter about courses, height, airspeed, weather, and so on. I feel that I should explain that we were veterans only on a survival basis. Our experience was limited, but we were alive to pass on even our small store of knowledge.

"We were going to a quiet little spot called Lorient on that occasion, and, barring errors of navigation (my depart-ment) which might put us over a heavily defended area, we anticipated no bother.

"Other people, we knew had been to Lorient and had not come back, but that sort of thing was not for us. How cocky could you get on the strength of just three trips?

"At 4.55 on that January afternoon, our two motors poured life into Wellington 'Z for Zebra', and whatever we had omitted to do must wait five hours or so, for we were airborne. Carl Taylor, our 'driver-airframe' (who had the thoroughly-approved-by-all ambition to return to Pensacola, in the US of A, to meet the USAAF pilot who had checked him out as unsuitable for flying heavy aircraft) set our first course on his compass. I settled down to try and make sure that he flew that course. That was a conflict of skills which finally generated quite astonishing flying.

"From the point of view of operational flying, the flight to target and return passed without incident.

"The bombardier, Don Mortimer, was the busiest bloke on board, spotting for landmarks to assist my navigation; pumping oil on the well-known Zwicky hand pump at necessary intervals; checking his bombsight, his front gun-turret; standing by for that moment that always caused my heart to miss a beat—when we changed off from overload to main petrol tanks. We had a good idea when this was due and Don would stand by the change-over cocks. We always flew till the motors checked in their steady beat, then over to main tanks whereupon the motors roared on. Even a not very keen ear would have heard us all start breathing again. We were a pretty average crew, so I expect that reaction was general.

"Lorient came, bombs went down, flak came up, Lorient went. Some days before we had done the same trip, and a very keen and accurate battery at Lannion, near the French coast, had nearly 'got the coconut'. This time we were very alert and on course, and speed, and time-at-turning-point out of target. I like to think it was all very efficient and impressive to our pupil pilot.

"We settled to the routine of going home, and I, as a keen navigator, decided to improve the hour with a bit of astro-navigation—taking sextant shots of the stars (definitely all the rage then). I passed the course to fly along with the pilot's time at our turning point for course alteration to base; I also indicated a

The crew after being posted to RAF Leeming and re-equipped with Halifax BVs. Here they have the addition of a flight engineer and a mid-upper gunner. Three of the original crew who crashed in Wellington X3348 are: D. Mortimer, bomb aimer (*second from left*); C. Taylor, pilot; D. Martin, navigator. The wireless operator, W. (Taffy) Baker, on the extreme right missed the Lorient raid and the resulting crash because of a heavy cold.

couple of light beacons close to our route, which would help them to pinpoint our position.

"Well there I was, the very model of a good navigator, practising to improve his skill, when the drivers reported a cloud ahead, and said that they would let down through and it. I returned to my 'office' to check our position once more, to look out for any discernible landmark and to work on my first 'star fix'. The bombardier went into the front turret so as to get the clearest, earliest view of whatever might be visible and useful to us in fixing our position.

"Almost at once we began flying in cloud, which was patchy in areas, and suddenly a light beacon was seen flashing below. The identification letter, flashed in Morse, was intermittent and none too clear, but we all finally agreed upon an ID letter. Although, if what was seen was accurately identified, that put us some fifty miles ahead of where my dead-reckoning suggested. My own opinion of my navigation was such that it did not cause me much surprise. I forgot that useful maxim, 'believe nothing you hear, and only half of what you see', and proceeded to give the course change to take us to base. I assured the pilots that it was alright to continue to lose height through the cloud, which completely enshrouded us, as we should be over the plains leading to north Yorkshire.

"Flying in cloud had a timeless quality so I cannot even guess how long we continued to descend, but when our altimeter showed 1,400 feet Carl decided to climb out of it, just in case we were not where we thought we were, but somewhere near higher ground. Then it happened.

"I was sitting on the floor, with my back towards the bulkhead door of the pilots' compartment. The wireless operator amazed me by beating his head on his set. I can remember thinking that being annoyed because the set would not function properly was one thing, but to vent one's wrath by beating one's head on the thing was going a bit too far.

"My attention was drawn to heather and herbage coming up through the floor, which hardly seemed consistent with flying through cloud, no matter how thick. It was about that time that it dawned on me that I had been sitting at my table, which now seemed to have adopted a rather odd angle—I definitely could not recall getting up and leaving it. The motors had ceased their monotonous roar and the noise had been replaced instead with a crackling and hissing. Coupled with that was the smell of hot oil and hot metal.

"Suddenly and simultaneously the wireless operator, with bleeding face and I without a scratch, realised that we had crashed, and sitting around was no way to react. We both got moving towards the astrodome, which doubled as an escape hatch. I was suprised to meet another fellow there, for we only had a rear gunner, but such is the state of one's mind at such a time that it did not occur to me that he too might be looking for the exit.

"After what seemed like tens of minutes, during which the crackling seemed ever more ominous, we got the hatch open and shot out of that hole like pips out of a gooseberry. We found the two pilots already out and getting organised on the rescue of the bombardier from the front turret.

"In all our minds was the fear of a sudden explosion into fire that usually accompanied such accidents as ours, and the problem of how to get him out looked almost impossible to solve.

"The turret looked as though some giant had gripped it with one hand at the bottom and the other at the top and just wrung it like a dishcloth. What with the twisting and the gun breeches in there, the only evidence that there was room for a man was the fact that he was there—

unconscious but alive. He was lying so oddly that it seemed that he must have been broken in many places.

"Still there was the crackling and fizzing from the motors. It was dark, wet and cold.

"I never did know, and never was able to recall, how we managed to get him out. We worked in a sort of controlled frenzy, trying not to hurry so much as to make any injuries worse, yet not so slowly so as to be caught halfway through the job by the expected fire. I know that it did occur to us that if his legs were broken it would make his extraction easier, if we could get a big enough gap to get his head and shoulders through.

"At last we did manage to make such a gap and suddenly he was free. We hurriedly carried him away from that crackling plane.

"The mist began to clear somewhat and we could see the aircraft sitting on the ground in a flying position, quite level. Also, as our frightened ears calmed down, we found that the noises were getting less and less threatening. After a while we became convinced that the risk of fire had diminished sufficiently to return to the shelter of the fuselage. There we wrapped Mortimer up as best we could from the raw cold. He lay quietly and we deduced that he was suffering from concussion along with severe injuries to his legs. We didn't probe about too much, as we didn't want to make his injuries worse—we did make sure that he wasn't badly gashed and losing blood.

"Where we were was anyone's guess; we could neither see nor hear anything. Someone had to stay with the injured bomb-aimer whilst others sought help. We discovered that between the six of us we had just one torch to light our way to civilisation.

"Someone thought of the Very pistol; so with my battledress blouse and pockets stuffed with cartridges, I and two others

Pilot Officer Martin, navigator

stood deciding which way to head into the darkness to find help.

"At that moment we heard a train—most certainly the most welcome train that ever there was—especially as we saw its fire. (Since then I have been able to accept any coincidence.) That blessed fireman chose to open the firebox door and bung in another shovelful of coal, just at the right moment. A noise can come from anywhere, but a pinprick of light, in almost impenetrable blackness, comes from one place and you can walk towards that place.

"In order to illuminate the ground around where we stood, I fired my first Very-light cartridge and we set off across the peaty soil that was criss-crossed with gullies. At least when we did fall, which was frequently, it was soft.

"The wireless operator, rear gunner and myself made up our little party. How we wished for another train to indicate the right direction, for no landmarks were discernible. A flare gives only limited light, and not for long.

"Shortly, we came to where the ground fell away sharply into the blackness. Several cartridges failed to show up any easy way downwards. Over we went, being as careful as we could, since we would not be much good with broken legs. Somehow we felt that if we broke our necks, then we would be excused, but to break a leg would have been silly and unforgivable. We tripped on rocks, fell into a stream (seemed like streams). We stumbled into cracks in the ground and slithered on our backs, fronts and sides, whichever happened to be in contact with the ground when we fell. I have a genius for landing myself with much toil in the course of trying to dodge it, and even on that occasion I managed to find time to practise.

"I came upon a broken-down, dry-stone wall and, looking up from the glen, into which we had stumbled, I saw what appeared to be a house gable-end showing up against the skyline. I climbed towards it to rouse the residents. Of course it didn't turn out to be a house—it was not even a barn, but rather it was just an odd arrangement of rocks. I slithered back down into the glen and discovered the stream once more. With my trousers amply filled with water, I found myself beyond profanity.

"Fortunately, the cartridges remained usable, and we continued our descent with the aid of their feeble glimmers. At last we stumbled upon a well-defined path and, some way along, fields . . . then, at last, a village.

"It was well past closing time and the local residents were all abed. Our calls brought forth no one and so we selected a door and proceeded to assault it. After a noticeable interval an upstairs window opened and we got a most welcome 'Who are you?'

"We announced our identities in heavy accents, Cockney (mine), and Geordie (rear gunner's) and we were accepted by our interrogator—who, after some delay decided that we were 'some of ours'. He opened up for us and invited us to go inside, whereupon he sent another member of the household to rouse the villagers and the local organisation for the defence of the realm.

"As it turned out we had arrived at a farmhouse in the village of Hope, in Edale, Derbyshire, some fifty miles off our course.

"In no time at all the fire was kindled and we were given a beer to tide us over until the kettle boiled. I was on the telephone to our base just in time to stop the 'we regret to inform you that your husband/son/father/brother has failed to return from operations' telegrams from being sent out (also forestalling the consumption of six rum rations, six servings of bacon and eggs—homing bait— by anyone who happened to be nearest to them). At the same time a party was being gathered to go up onto the moor and bring the pilots and poor Mortimer down.

"Incidentaly, in the course of conversation, we learned that our 'arrival' on the local hills had been heard, but past experience had taught them to wait until daylight before attempting a rescue. Trying to locate crash sites and survivors in the dark had always proved futile. It would appear that we were the first to come down under our own steam.

Wellington crash site—a few fragments remain.

"One of the assembling members of the search party was a local shepherd. Lean, weather-beaten, slow of speech, calm-mannered and quietly spoken, he cross-examined us on our route down from the moor. We gave him as much detail as we could (including my misbegotten clump of rocks) and at the end he declared that he thought that he knew of a path that would bring the search party to the plane.

"It was still dark as we set off, our

pathfinder leading the way with me behind him and then a stretcher party along with a doctor. The pace seemed almost leisurely, though perhaps my judgement was faulted by a desire to get help to Mortimer as quickly as possible; in any case, I soon found out that if I kept station with the leader, I would do very nicely.

"I suppose that there was a path; all I did was watch where the shepherd put his feet and put mine in the same places. After what seemed like an age of plodding we were up on the moor top, and looking around trying to spot the plane in the blackness. I knew that it was not much good me looking; when examined for my fitness in regards to aircrew, it was found that there were insufficient grades of 'night vision', so they crossed them all out and wrote 'poor'.

"We came to a sudden halt; the shepherd's confidence in his own powers was vindicated, for he pointed to a shape that didn't belong on the moor. It was our Wimpey, not more than a hundred yards ahead of the rescue party.

"The doctor's opinion of Mortimer's condition was encouraging, and Morty's spirit, now that he was conscious, was also heartening. What clinched it for me, and removed my worries regarding Morty's well-being, was the language he used during his observations of our attempts at stretcher-bearing on that return trip. It is a fact that if we hadn't had him securely lashed down, he would have been in the village before us.

"Notwithstanding the apparent slowness of our travel, the trip up the glen and down again had only taken about an hour, and there to meet us on our return was an ambulance ready to take the more seriously injured to hospital. The local organisation was right on the ball. The local hotelier had hot baths, meals and beds ready for those who were not so bent that nature couldn't do the straightening.

"When we woke next morning our clothes had been dried and there was good news concerning Morty in hospital. Don Mortimer, incredibly, had broken no bones, but had severely twisted both his ankles. To this day he still walks awkwardly, compared to the quick athletic step that was his prior to the accident. He came back and finished a tour of operations with us before going on to qualify as a pilot. On his second tour as pilot he got himself shot down. Having seen Morty in that twisted turret, I believe his survival to be one of the great marvels that I have ever been privileged to witness.

"Out of the nine aircraft detailed from 427 Squadron, eight dropped their bombs on Lorient from around 15,000 feet through ten-tenths cloud. All aircraft made it back to England, but had to land at various airfields, due to lack of fuel.

"'Z for Zebra' bounced along the only flat surface within ten miles when it struck the Derbyshire hills at Blackden Edge. The escape of all the crew members was considered so fortunate as to warrant a feature article in some Sunday newspapers, with such headings as: 'Pilot makes miraculous landing—million to one chance'."

So ends Pilot Officer Martin's account of his experiences on the Derbyshire hills. As for Wellington X3348, it was broken up and dragged off the moor—leaving a few metal fragments at the crash site.

The target, the French town of Lorients, along with another town housing U-boat pens, St Nazaire, were flattened. U-boats were to sit secure in their concrete pens until the following year, when a bomb was developed that would penetrate the reinforced concrete. The effects of those early raids on the Battle of the Atlantic amounted to no more than giving the U-boat crews some disturbed nights.

Thunderbolt P47C, 416297, 63 Fighter Squadron USAAF, flying from Horsham St Faith to Liverpool and return, crashed on Horsehill Tor, 25th April, 1943.

Map reference 094843• Map key number 31

It just didn't make any sense to the fighter pilots who were to fly this, the latest production from Republic Aviation, the P47 'Thunderbolt'. It weighed six tons; it looked big, fat and ugly to the american pilots who were used to the more sleekly designed Airocobras, Lightnings and the British Spitfire. Someone likened it to a jug—and the name stuck.

In April of 1943, a 'Jug' of 56 Fighter Group, 8th Airforce, power dived onto Horsehill Tor, Edale, during a thunderstorm. The pilot, Second-Lieutenant John E Coenen, baled out and sustained some spinal damage, but five months later went on to destroy two German aircraft, before being grounded and shipped back to the States, because of his injuries.

The previous year, June 1942, John E Coenen had graduated as a fighter pilot at the age of twenty-one, and after gaining experience on the new 'pursuit airplane', was assigned as a replacement pilot with 63 Fighter Squadron, 56 Fighter Group. The Group arrived in England on the *Queen Elizabeth* in January 1943.

In April, the Group was stationed at Horsham St Faith, Norwich. On Easter Sunday some parts were required from Liverpool. John 'Fatboy' Coenen, who had been made Assistant Operations Officer with 63 Squadron, volunteered to make the one hundred and eighty mile cross-country trip.

As Coenen swung the heavy fighter's nose around to face the runway at Horsham, gusts of wind shook and buffeted the Thunderbolt. It wasn't ideal weather for flying on that Easter Sunday in 1943, but then the weather over Britain was rarely ideal. In the three months of flying that Coenen and the rest of the pilots in 56 Group had undergone since their arrival, they had come to the conclusion that if you didn't fly in adverse weather conditions, then you didn't fly at all.

Coenen planned to make for an airfield close to the city of Liverpool where he hoped to find some transport to pick up the parts. After an uneventful flight he

Second Lieutenant John E. Coenen

reached his destination only to find that there were no vehicles available for him to use. Nor was public transport running because of the national holiday. Coenen took off once more, heading for another airfield closer to his intended destination.

Towards the evening he had the parts and was ready to make the return flight but the weather was taking a turn for the worse. Second-Lieutenant John E Coenen recalled that eventful trip:

"I tried to keep under the clouds, but pretty soon they were right down on the hills in the Manchester-Sheffield area. I decided to climb above the huge thunderheads, which were piling up over the centre of England. I had started a normal climb, and was right in among the thunder clouds, when suddenly my 'plane began bucking and being tossed around like a cork on the ocean.

"I lost all sense of direction and at one point found myself hanging upside-down from my seat straps. Then the 'plane fell into a spin, and I knew that under ideal conditions it took from two to three thousand feet to pull a P47 out of a spin. I knew that I must be almost on top of the hills—I would never pull out in time. As far as I could see, the 'plane was a goner—I had to get out and fast.

"Thrusting back the canopy and unstrapping myself, I stood on the seat and attempted to jump, but found that I couldn't move—maybe the spin was responsible. I don't remember pulling the ripcord, but I guess that I must have done, for I was torn away from the cockpit, and looking up I could see the parachute canopy opening up above me—one panel of which was missing, and another ripped. I was coming down much too fast."

At Upper Booth in the Vale of Edale inhabitants were brought from their houses by a high-pitched roar in the rain-soaked clouds. Bernard Taylor and his friends were out hiking that day, and were sheltering from the thunderstorm in a house near the end of the valley, where the path called 'Jacob's Ladder' was situated. They ran out and were in time to hear the impact as the heavy fighter slammed into Dale Head—below Horsehill Tor. They watched as a fire blazed furiously up at the crash site. The sound of exploding .50 ammunition echoed down the valley. Then, as they were looking upwards, they saw the rapidly descending parachute of the pilot.

Coenen hit—square on the path, landing awkwardly and heavily before being dragged a short distance by his 'chute.

Mr Taylor reached the pilot first; Coenen was groaning with pain. He asked the American to try and move his legs, to see if his spine had been damaged by his heavy landing. John Coenen knew that he had been hurt pretty badly and at first wouldn't allow the hikers to move him.

Spotting a five-barred gate the hikers, led by Mr Taylor, took it off its hinges and used it as a stretcher to move the pilot into nearby 'Lee House'.

Mr Taylor, of Didsbury, Manchester, remembered the events of that evening:

"We had to ascertain whether or not the pilot was flying alone, because anyone who may have baled out with him could have drifted onto Kinder Scout plateau, a most inhospitable place to spend a stormy night. After making him as comfortable as we could we chased down to the Church House at Edale and telephoned the police at Hope.

"Next morning we climbed across to the crash site. The fighter had buried itself into the side of the hill; all around lay exploded cartridges."

John Coenen had fractured the eleventh and twelfth dorsal vertebrae of his backbone. Four and a half months later the pilot from Oklahoma returned to his squadron in 56 Fighter Group and into action. Up to the time of his crash he had only flown one sortie, and that was of short duration over the Dutch estuaries.

Three 'jugs' in dark green camouflage paint; the light painted nose ring was to clearly distinguish the Thunderbolt from the German FW190.

Back once again at his squadron he was experiencing some pain in his back, especially when he pulled the Jug into a tight turn. On some occasions the pain became so great that it caused him to break formation. When coming up against the Luftwaffe breaking formation was a dangerous procedure, for it meant leaving the protective covering fire of your own fighters. He put the pain down to weak muscles, through being laid up in hospital, and he exercised daily to try and put matters right.

During the spring and summer of 1943, the Americans stepped up their deep, daylight penetration bombing raids into Germany; as a consequence, losses for the 'Mighty Eighth' mounted. Steps were afoot to provide the Flying Fortresses and Liberators with fighter cover all the way to the target, and back. On 27th September, Thunderbolt fighters, using drop tanks, were to escort the bombers to ward off the hordes of Me 109s and FW 190s.

The target was Emden, which meant that the fighters faced a two-hundred mile journey over the North Sea. The trip was made possible by using seventy-five gallon drop tanks. Coenen's squadron was to be part of that escort, shepherding and protecting the second task force.

On that September morning the

Thunderbolt in natural metal finish with underslung fuel drop-tanks that extended its range, enabling it to operate deep into Germany.

weather was what the Americans had come to expect—cloudy and overcast. The fighters climbed to 24,000 feet and set out to rendezvous with the B17s off the Frisian Islands. Because of the rapidly deteriorating weather conditions, the fighters of 56 Group failed to link up with their charges. It was only after the bombers had completed the raid on Emden that the Thunderbolts picked them up and took up protective positions above the formations.

Coenen was positioned last in a box of four fighters of 63 Squadron—they were out to the right of the B17s. That position placed Coenen at the extreme rear. As the raiders headed out over the sea, Coenen was last man out of Germany. This was his thirteenth mission since returning to his squadron, and it was to be his last.

They were at 24,000 feet when Coenen's flight leader, Captain Vogt, spotted some unidentified aircraft below them—they appeared to be heading towards the bombers. Leading his flight of four Jugs, Captain Vogt descended to investigate. As they closed in, the unidentified aircraft took shape, they were Focke-Wulf FW190s, six of them. As Vogt led his flight into a turning circle with the six 'butcherbirds', Coenen

Air to air photograph of 63 Squadron.

spotted another nine of them racing in from the left to join the fray. The odds were four to one against the Americans —they needed help. All attempts to bring assistance, however, were thwarted by some effective jamming of the Allied radios by German ground control.

John Coenen was suffering increasing pain in his back as he was forced to pull hard on the control column to keep formation in the turning circle with the more manoeuvrable FW190s. The torture became unbearable and on the point of passing out, he broke away to the opposite side of the circle—usually a fatal thing to do but he could not help it as the pain was too great.

With the fighter trimmed for turns, immediately upon him breaking the turn the nose reared up and the FWs began to turn inside him, intent upon making him their first victim.

Seeing Coenen's plight, Vogt and his Number 2 pitched into the FW190s closing in on Coenen. Number 3 was not seen to go down to the German fighters, but he must have been hit first, for none of the others saw him again after they broke circle to assist Coenen.

For Coenen, the pain lessened as he levelled off at 25,000 feet, but the nippy FW190s had stayed with him and were closing in for the kill. Suddenly, an FW190 flashed in front of him—the pilot had obviously misjudged his own speed in his eagerness to score against the 'sitting duck'. It was an opportunity Coenen could not afford to miss—having resigned himself to being shot down, he had decided to try and 'throw a little lead' before they got him.

Realising his mistake the German pilot began to pull a tight turn towards the Thunderbolt, but in doing so presented an excellent target. With his first burst Coenen raked the fuselage along the left side. The eight machine guns put up a devastating fuselade, and he watched in wonder as his second burst sprayed along both wings taking in the cockpit. The pilot must have been hit for the Focke-Wulf settled back and no evasive action was taken as Coenen closed in and set it aflame with a third burst.

As could happen in dog-fights of the Second World War, one minute a particular part of the sky could be filled with aircraft twisting and turning in general confusion and the next minute there were hardly any aircraft in sight. Coenen had watched his victim spinning away down through the clouds, some 5,000 feet below, trailing smoke—he was alone.

Above him and in the distance he could see two unmistakable robust shapes— Thunderbolts. If he could tag onto them he might stand a chance of getting home. As he began to overhaul them, he noted another radial engine fighter apparently intent upon catching the two P47 Thunderbolts, only this one sported a bright yellow paint job around the nose —it was a Focke-Wulf 190.

The eerie whining whistle in his earphones told Coenen that the Germans were still engaged in jamming—he had no way of warning the two American fighters.

Glancing round to make sure that there were no German fighters stalking him, he opened up the throttle. The P47 Thunderbolt was notoriously slow off the mark because of the enormous bulk, but once it got moving the speed gradually built up until it could outpace any German operational fighter at that period. Within minutes Coenen had come within range of the stalking FW190, the pilot of which was too intent upon bagging his two fat prey to notice the Thunderbolt tucked in under his condensation trail.

At seventy-five yards Coenen squeezed the trigger on the control column and the fighter in his sights 'lit up like a Christmas tree'. It spun away earth-

wards, the German pilot making no attempt to get out.

Coenen felt a surge of satisfaction as he recognised the code letters on the two unsuspecting Thunderbolts—it was Vogt and his Number 2—he had come to their rescue and returned a favour.

That day 63 Fighter Squadron had scored five victories; Number 3 in Vogt's flight was the only casualty. The Thunderbolts of 56 Fighter Group had flown four-hundred miles, mostly over water, and had inflicted a defeat on the Luftwaffe of twenty-one to one. Two of the enemy had fallen to Second-Lieutenant John E Coenen, but his elation was short-lived. After a medical examination he was declared unfit for flying and was grounded due to severe spinal injuries; damage sustained when he dropped out of the skies over Derbyshire. He was awarded the Air Medal and two clusters, then sent home to recuperate.

Thunderbolt scraps where the fighter impacted with the ground on Horsehill Tor.

Liberator PB4Y-1 63949, VB110 Bombing Squadron, United States Navy, Dunkeswell, returning from Bay of Biscay patrol, abandoned over Lincolnshire, crashed at Broken Ground, 18th December, 1943.

Map reference 008015 ● Map key number 32

It was a particularly bad night as Mr Utton walked along the blacked-out road from Stalybridge to Millbrook. It was going on for nine o'clock, seven days before Christmas, 1943.

Above the wind he heard the heavy drone of an aircraft approaching from the south-west and flying along the valley in his direction—it sounded to be very low. Suddenly, a huge, black shape, darker than the surrounding night, roared into view passing a mere three hundred feet above the chimneys of Hartshead Power Station. Mr Utton stared after it in amazement as it lumbered on up the valley and was swallowed up by the blackness. Did the crew realise just how low they were? Did they know of the high ground lying directly ahead of them? It seemed to him that there was something seriously wrong. Had he been able to see inside the four-engined bomber he would

have been even more surprised—and alarmed.

Tucked into the bomb bay of the PB4Y-1 (Consolidated Liberator) of the United States Navy were sixteen depth charges, each consisting of 250 lb of torpex high explosive.

Nothing stirred within the ponderous, box-shaped fuselage of the aircraft, every crew position was unoccupied, including the 1st and 2nd pilots' positions. The anti-submarine bomber was deserted and flying on automatic pilot. A wrecked radar set, deliberately destroyed by an explosive charge, was the only sign of damage. Fuel gauges on the pilots' instrument panel were registering zero, and had been for the past fifteen minutes or so. The starboard outer engine had been the first to falter and stop. With no pilot's hand to press the feathering button, the huge propeller continued to 'windmill' causing sufficient drag to pull the doomed bomber off its pre-set course; thus causing it to turn away from the heavily populated area of Lancashire.

Who had set that lethal flying bomb lumbering across industrial England, and why?

It was fourteen hours earlier, at 7 o'clock that morning, when PB4Y-1 63949 took off from RAF Dunkeswell in Devon for a routine patrol over the Bay of Biscay. At the controls was Lieutenant George Charno, United States Naval Reserve; sitting beside him in the second pilot's seat was co-pilot Robert G Wissman, Lieutenant, junior grade. Along with them were eight other crew members plus a passenger; a total complement of eleven USN flyers. Four other PB4Y-1s of Bombing Squadron 110, were on anti-submarine patrol that morning of the 18th December; none of them would make it back to their base at Dunkeswell.

Two months earlier, Bombing Squadron VB110 had become a part of the Battle of the Atlantic, which had its beginnings three years previously on August 17th, 1940. when the German Reich announced a total blockade of the British Isles. Britain was going to be starved into submission by cutting off her sea links with the USA. That cutting off was to be accomplished by Admiral Doenitz's U-Boats.

With the fall of France, the Kriegsmarine secured bases on the Bay of Biscay coastline from where they could sail to intercept the massive convoys of merchant ships crossing the Atlantic. By mid-1942, the U-Boats were gaining the upper hand, as they hunted and attacked in packs. Battles would last for days and sometimes it meant destruction for a whole convoy.

The tide of the Battle of the Atlantic turned in 1943 with the arrival of long-range aircraft and their use in ever increasing numbers. Operating with powerful radar sets, they began to locate and sink U-Boats in growing numbers.

The Bay of Biscay was an ideal location to catch the submarines as they set out from, or returned to, the security of their concrete pens at Brest, St Nazaire and Lorient. It was whilst U-Boats were crossing the Bay of Biscay for the open Atlantic, that Coastal Command worked hard to keep them submerged, thus decreasing the endurance of their batteries, making the U-Boats less effective in the shipping lanes. During the Summer of 1943, twenty U-Boats had been destroyed in the Bay of Biscay. However, RAF Coastal Command was under pressure from the Luftwaffe operating from airfields in Brittany. Help was on its way in the form of USN anti-submarine units. In July 1943, in the United States, a new squadron was being formed—it was to be designated 'Patrol Squadron VB-110'. Among the pilots who volunteered to be part of that new squadron, was Joe Kennedy, elder brother of the late John F Kennedy, ex-President of the United States.

On the trip across the Atlantic to the United Kingdom Joe Kennedy's 'plane and that of the crew of 63949 piloted by Charno, kept company arriving at St Eval, Cornwall, via Greenland. After completing the usual acclimatisation, VB110 Squadron moved to Dunkeswell in Devon, and was readied for operations against the U-Boat menace.

Patrols were up to twelve hours long and were most uncomfortable for the crews. Towards the rear of the PB4Y it was icy cold, and yet in the cockpit it could become like an oven. Meals on the long patrols consisted of coffee and sandwiches, eaten whilst the crew scoured the skies for German fighters and the ocean for U-Boats. By December the weather was appalling and Dunkeswell lay in a covering of snow. But the constant patrols seemed to be keeping the U-Boats beneath the surface in the Bay

Setting off for a patrol over the Bay of Biscay.

IMPERIAL WAR MUSEUM

of Biscay; so when the weather was good enough at dawn for take-off, regardless of what threatened in the way of weather for the evening, the patrols set out. Consequently, whenever the weather worsened, returning aircraft had to seek out airfields where they stood a chance of getting down in one piece.

On the morning of 18th December, at 4 am, George Charno joined his co-pilot in the freezing aerology hut, along with Joe Kennedy and three other pilots and their co-pilots. Five aircraft were scheduled to go on patrol over 'U-Boat Alley'. They listened as the weather officer predicted a cold front moving in from the west that would effectively close Dunkeswell at 5.30 pm; about the time that they were due to return.

Despite that disquieting bit of information, no move was made to scrub the operation and eventually the crews filed into the flight mess for the traditional pre-flight breakfast of steak and eggs.

At 7 am it was still dark as Charno lifted the PB4Y from the runway and pointed its nose to the west. The Cornish coastline passed beneath them and the navigator gave the course change that would place them over their assigned patrol area 'Percussion T-4'. The weather was atrocious, with clouds down to four hundred feet in places and winds gusting at fifty knots. Visibility was poor and adding to the crew's lack of vision was the heavy condensation forming on the aircraft's plexiglass. George Charno opted to carry out the patrol at 1,500 feet, up in the overcast. The probing radar beam would pick up anything moving on the ocean's surface in their area.

Patrolling another allotted section of the Bay, Joe Kennedy began his search below the clouds and was forced into wave hopping, as the gale force winds whipped the sea into a near storm.

The morning dragged on for the crews and at 11 am a radio message was received from 19 Group, back at Dunkeswell, informing them that the expected bad weather front was moving into the British Isles faster than earlier predicted. All patrolling PB4Ys were to return to base by 5 pm. George Charno in 63949 had been expecting that recall and had allowed for it in his plotted sweep.

On the return trip, the weather seemed to improve as they neared the Cornish coast; but they could see coming in behind them a huge bad weather front. Dunkeswell lay shrouded in heavy cloud and drizzle. With visibility down to 1,400 yards, the controller decided to divert the five returning U-Boat hunters to RAF Beaulieu, near Southampton.

PB4Y 63949 made landfall at Bude Bay and dropped low enough to keep visual contact with the ground—it was a straight run home. Their flight path took them over Winkleigh Airfield, but as they had received no communication that their base at Dunkeswell was 'out', they continued on.

Whilst still homing on the radio beacon at Dunkeswell, they received instructions to divert to Beaulieu, some seventy-five miles to the east in a direct line. Passing over their base the co-pilot suggested that they put down at home — although conditions were not the best. However, Charno reasoned that Beaulieu must be clear and safe so why should they take unnecessary risks? Anyway, they had received their orders.

The navigator, Ensign Cecil R Colyer, altered course for Beaulieu and the radioman changed frequency to pick up that airfield. He then proceeded to request altimeter setting and cloud base, from the controller at Beaulieu.

Visibility was becoming increasingly reduced as heavy condensation began to build up and darkness fell. Charno pulled the PB4Y up to 1,500 feet and flew on instruments, arriving over Beaulieu at 5 pm.

The approach was frustrating, for as they were coming in towards the field on what was known as QGH (a procedure for bringing in aircraft in unfavourable conditions), radio messages were up to five minutes late in arriving; this was because of communication congestion due to other aircraft. But at last they were in a position to begin landing procedure according to the message they were receiving.

PB4Y 63949 dropped through the cloud base to 800 feet—no sign of landing lights.

"Turn back west—we've missed the field!" called the wireless operator.

Cursing, Charno dipped the port wing and began to turn back onto a westerly heading.

"Barrage balloons!" came the cry from co-pilot Robert Wissman.

A low whistle in the earphones signalled the truth of his warning — they were roaring through a vast forest of balloon cables, and picking up the avoidance signals from them.

"Must be Southampton," muttered Charno, as he turned the bomber south and headed it away from the danger area.

The PB4Y's radio was crackling and spluttering as hail and rain lashed the aircraft. Over the air, frantic calls of other 'planes in trouble could be heard, as they also tried to establish their positions.

Co-pilot, Lieutenant Wissman, added his voice to the urgent radio chatter, informing flying control that they had been in the air twelve hours and were running short of gas. The cockpit seemed to crowd in on the two pilots and the temperature inside was climbing higher—the windows streamed with condensation.

Another radio signal from flying

control at Beaulieu—should they use it and try a blind approach on that beam?

"Let's make for the south coast—I think I can find the field myself, once I know exactly where we are," snapped Wissman.

Ignoring the radio signals they headed due south. Suddenly, they were at the coast and with every crew member peering earthwards, they were able to identify their position exactly.

"Portsmouth!" came a triumphant cry.

"Now just leave it to me!" Snapped Wissman determindly as he took over the controls. With the starboard wing well down, the co-pilot stared out into the gloom, and thanks to the white foam lashing the coast and beaches, he was able to pick out the Isle of Wight. Sticking to the coastline he brought the PB4Y to the northern-most tip, then crossed the Solent.

"Keep your eyes peeled for the inlet of the River Beaulieu!" he called to the men peering through the aircraft's nose."

Once more they managed to contact flying control: "For Pete's sake, turn on the damned airdrome lights!" yelled Charno.

Unhurriedly and coolly the reply came back from Beaulieu, "All runway lights are on."

In the bomber they could see nothing through the rain squalls. Once they had picked up the river estuary, it should have been easy—Beaulieu aerodrome lay a short way to the west, about two miles up the inlet. At least they now knew where they were as they followed the river. Then came the news over the radio that there was an obstruction directly in their flight path, and a safe height was suggested.

"Incredible!" gasped Wissman in loud disbelief, as he pulled hard back on the controls and took the bomber back into the black overcast.

"That does it—how are we supposed to get down now?"

"We'll try on QDM again. Flying control can get us down," snapped Charno as he took over the controls once more. "Initiate QDM letdown procedure", he called to his radioman.

"We've been instructed to hold—there are other 'planes in circuit" replied the radioman—the irritation in his voice was all too apparent as he manipulated his

A weather-beaten PB4Y at Dunkeswell

67

spluttering apparatus.

The two pilots began to calculate their remaining flying time, and concluded that they had sufficient fuel for three hours. It was about 6 pm and completely dark.

They continued flying on a northerly heading for a short time, turned and began flying west and east, alternatively. They timed their turns and flight durations to maintain a position to the north of Beaulieu.

"OK! It's our turn!" yelled the radioman. "Beaulieu wish to commence QGH procedure with us. Go to 1,700 feet."

The pilot eased the bomber down gently through the clouds and suddenly froze. Balloon whistles filled his earphones as he quickly brought PB4Y around to 090 degrees. He didn't dare climb for fear of colliding with one of the other 'planes circling above.

"I can't hold the signal," the radioman called, his voice filled with urgency. He was having increasing difficulty tuning the overheating transmitter—the smell of hot bakerlite filled the cockpit. What with the weather playing havoc with the antennae, and the constant, near-frantic use the set was getting, it seemed that it was on the point of packing in altogether.

It was pointless carrying on with the airfield approach, so Charno recommenced flying the east-west pattern. Using the command set, he began to employ the 'Darky' system (code name for emergency radio transmission signals to call for assistance) and succeeded in getting an answer—but, it was too garbled and unreadable. Charno, the co-pilot Wissman, and the navigator continued to call Darky for the remainder of the flight, but received no further answer.

They were in serious trouble and turned their IFF (Identification Friend or Foe) system to 'emergency'.

"We have Beaulieu again, and they are recommending a QGH," called the radioman.

"This is it . . . we're going in and to hell with the damned balloons." snapped Charno, who was convinced that they were far enough away from Southampton to worry about the warning whistles.

"It's gone, I've lost the signal!" cried the near-distraught radioman, who was frantically twiddling the knobs on his set, "It's conked out."

It was 6.30 pm.

At about that time, Joe Kennedy swept in through the wind and rain, aided by flares, and put his PB4Y down at Beaulieu aerodrome. As he taxied his weary aircraft off the runway, the control tower was sending up flares to try and guide 63949 to safety.

At one point the crew thought that they saw flares, but were unable to develop the sightings.

It had become obvious that the set would never work again and once more Charno let down through the overcast, and ordered the crew to keep lookout through the two after hatches. They were to look out for airfield lights, beacons, searchlights, anything that would help them pinpoint their position.

"Lights!" came the cry from the co-pilot's seat.

Sure enough, a long straight stretch of twin lights lay beneath them.

"It's got to be a runway — it sure looks like one." Called Wissman, hopefully. Charno lined up the lights and began an approach.

"Climb! Climb! screamed a voice on the intercom. "For Pete's sake . . . climb!"

Without asking for an explanation (the urgency in the navigator's voice didn't encourage questions) Charno, yet again, pushed the throttles open and zoomed for the clouds.

"Convoy — it was a convoy of army lorries," the navigator cried hoarsely. "We must have scared 'em half to death!"

They were not the only ones, was the

VIA BARRY BLUNT

Meeks Field, Iceland, 1st October, 1943, Charno's crew and two passengers on a flight leg to England. *Back row standing left to right:* R. G. Wissman, co-pilot; C. R. Colyer, navigator; G. H. Charno, pilot; W. O. Levering; D. S. Peterson; Sheely; W. W. Olson. *Front row:* Clyde Zappa, Squadron Leading Chief; Inman, passenger; W. J. Clayton; D. M. Clark.

unanimous thought of all on board the bomber.

They were running short on fuel, the weather was worsening, they didn't know their position for sure, and the radio was out. There was nothing left for them to do but abandon the aircraft. Charno spiralled to 5,000 feet above the position that they had last seen the convoy. Once they were well above the clouds he turned in a northerly direction.

None of the crew had ever jumped before and from a height of 5,000 feet they continued to peer down at the rainswept earth, praying for runway lights.

At 7.45 pm Charno gave the order to destroy the radar gear. The navigator organised the crew in preparation for them to jump, giving them instructions in a calm voice, hoping to appease their fears. But a number of them were scared and the inevitable happened — one of the crew yanked at his ripcord and his 'chute filled the after-station with silk. His buddies bundled it up and stuffed it into his arms; it was no time for niceties.

At 8 pm the navigator reported that all members of the crew were ready to jump. The one with the unpacked 'chute was the first to be hustled through the hatch by his fellow airmen and he fell into the night. One by one, each member of the crew followed, until by 8.15 pm they had all departed through the tunnel hatch leaving Wissman and Charno. Wissman ducked down into the nose and dropped through the nose-wheel door.

It had been a bad day, and it wasn't over yet, Charno had still one more job to do before he got out. The IFF equipment had to be destroyed by a small explosive charge. Turning the bomber onto a heading of 290 degrees, he set the automatic pilot and proceeded to destroy the last piece of secret equipment, then he too left through the nose-wheel door.

The whole crew landed in Lincolnshire, a short distance from the Wash; apart from some scratches and bruises, they were all down safe and sound. They were one hundred and fifty miles north of their intended landing place in the south of England.

Meanwhile, without a crew, the depth-charge laden bomber droned on over the centre of England, with sufficient potential in its belly to destroy a whole town centre.

Just short of Manchester, the last dregs of fuel were burned up in the starboard outer, Twin Wasp, radial engine and it spluttered into silence. The automatic pilot, unable to compensate for the enormous amount of drag exerted by the windmilling propellor, permitted the 'flying bomb' to enter a terminal, clockwise circuit losing height gradually.

It thundered along the Tame River Valley. Workers at Hartshead Power Station rushed out in time to see the huge roaring, black shape almost scrape the station's chimneys before it was swallowed up in the wintry night.

With speed reducing constantly, the PB4Y, still turning to starboard, crossed over the town of Mossley and thudded into the hard grit-covered moor known as Broken Ground, some 1,500 feet above sea level. There was no fire—there was no fuel left to burn. Because of the relatively soft crash-landing, the high explosives failed to go off, despite the fact that many of the depth charges had tumbled out onto the moor.

The following day local people went up to examine the American Navy bomber. John Mason, who was thirty-eight years old at the time of the crash, was the local gamekeeper for that stretch of moor and conscientiously mounted guard throughout the following night. However, when a contingent of US servicemen arrived to take over, their diligence left a lot to be desired. In no time at all some of the locals had stripped the wreck of valuable articles, the radio transmitter being among the first items

A USAAF Liberator in the same nose-down position that PB4Y-1 63934 USN ended up in.

to disappear. A demolition team arrived and exploded the depth charges. Later, PB4Y-1 63949 was broken up by a local man and sold for scrap. A few of the heavier objects remain at the site.

Charno, pilot of PB4Y-1 63949, was commended by Commodore Hamilton, Commander Fleet Air Wing Seven, for 'Taking correct and decisive action in an emergency and for the obvious good discipline of the crew.' What would have happened if the starboard engine had kept running just a few minutes longer, can only be surmised. Or if an engine on the port side had failed, the aircraft would have ended up circling Stockport and Manchester, gradually losing height with little possibility of a soft deposit for its lethal cargo.

It is of interest to note that six months later, the Americans were to formulate a plan to use an explosive-packed Liberator bomber against the enemy. German V weapon launching sites on the French coast were selected as targets, and a special force SAU-1 (Special Attack Unit) was formed at Dunkeswell. It was a volunteer force and the volunteers were drawn from crews of VB-110 Navy Squadron. Among the first to volunteer was Lieutenant Joe Kennedy, son of the former Ambassador to Britain, Joseph P Kennedy.

Joe Junior, had seen his younger brother John F Kennedy, win fame as a Navy Motor Torpedo Boat Commander in the Pacific — a naval hero who had saved his crew when a Japanese destroyer chopped his boat in half. In the anti-submarine war Joe Junior had failed to score, and turning down a proffered desk job, he volunteered to fly a worn-out Liberator, stripped of all guns and equipment and packed with 21,170 lb of torpex, towards a target on the French coast. The idea was for him to get the flying bomb airborne, put it on course for the target, set the arming solenoid, then bale out near Dover. Another aircraft, using radio control, would guide the crewless flying bomb and cause it to dive onto the target, where, it was hoped, it would explode and destroy the enemy 'terror weapon' installation.

On 12th August, 1944, a Liberator packed with explosives, took off with Joe Junior at the controls, but before it reached the British coastline and still over this Country, it mysteriously blew up killing Joe Kennedy and his volunteer co-pilot, 'Bud' Willy. The project was finally abandoned in favour of other more reliable methods.

By the end of the war, Navy Squadron VB110, based at Dunkeswell, had lost sixty-eight men killed. Two aircraft were lost to enemy fighters while on anti-submarine patrol over the Bay of Biscay and ten aircraft to mechanical failure or bad weather—the remains of one of these lies on Broken Ground, at the edge of the Peak District.

Ken Kershaw (to whom both *Dark Peak Aircraft Wrecks* books are dedicated) at the crash site, Broken Ground.

Spitfire P7883, 53 Operational Training Unit, Hibalstow; practising formation flying, crashed above Barber Booth, 10th December, 1943.

Map reference 108834 • Map key number 33

The hospital ward looked strange and different to the young flight sergeant as he slowly opened his eyes. A throbbing pain in his head reminded him of what he was doing there—a head on crash with another Spitfire, but there was something not quite right. There was a dream-like quality about the whole situation, as if he had slept for a long time. For example, the beds were different, he seemed to be facing the wrong wall, and he didn't recognise the ones around him in the other beds. He came to the conclusion that he had been moved during the night. But something else was puzzling him—his injuries. His amazing escape from the blazing Spitfire which crash-landed heavily, had left him with two fractured legs, fractured spine, broken nose and one broken arm. Somehow his injuries seemed to have healed miraculously. Maybe, he reasoned, he had suffered some sort of relapse; perhaps he was emerging from a coma.

The last thing he could remember was lying in a hospital bed at Larbart in Scotland, however, the nurse had just informed him that he was in a hospital in Buxton, Derbyshire—and that over two hundred miles away to the south.

Outside the windows he could see that it was wintertime, people around him were discussing Christmas, and yet surely, it should have been Easter. What, he wondered, had happened to the summer of '43?

"You've been involved in an accident," a nurse kindly explained. "You crashed in your Spitfire."

"Yes, I know," he replied. Ron Mitchell, the young pilot still felt that his mind was in chaos. Nothing seemed to make sense: he was in the wrong place . . . at the wrong time . . . and even more disturbing, with the wrong injuries.

That evening he received a visit from his father and at last the truth began to emerge. At first, his conversation with his father seemed to be at cross-purposes.

"You crashed twice—not once, don't you remember?"

Flight Lieutenant David Crichton was

the RAF doctor who had been involved in the fighter pilot's rescue from the Derbyshire moorland. It was the same David Crichton who was the pioneer founder of the Mountain Rescue Service. Stationed at RAF Harpur Hill, Buxton, the doctor was in the thick of it when it came to high ground aircraft crashes. It was Doctor Crichton who was able to fill in the missing gap in Ron Mitchell's memory—seven months in fact.

In March, 1943, Ron Mitchell had been stationed at Grangemouth, Scotland, with 53 Operational Training Unit, after returning from Canada where he had trained as a pilot.

On the afternoon of 18th March, he took off in a Spitfire Mk1B to practise some formation flying; he could recall the details vividly. He had formated on the port side of the flight leader, in the number three position, and in line with him was another Spitfire at number two position. Behind him and bringing up the rear was a fourth Spitfire in position four. The idea was to try to hold formation on the leader, the chief flying instructor, while he seemed hell-bent on ridding himself of the three fledglings. That was known as 'tail chasing'.

They began a steep climb through some heavy cumulus clouds. Ron Mitchell watched as the newer model Spitfire of the leader began to pull away. It was all right for the instructor tearing upwards like that, but his trainees in their older Mk1s were struggling to keep up. Ron Mitchell had the throttle wide open and was watching the speedo creep forward until it reached 160 mph.

Glancing up from his instrument panel he froze. A dark shape was hurtling down out of the clouds towards him. He barely had time to make out the shape of another Spitfire—a split second before it smacked into his port side with a mighty bang. Engine cowling whipped away in the slipstream and the huge black hulk of his Rolls-Royce Merlin engine reared up before him as it tore free from its mountings and plunged earthwards.

Flames shot out from the forty-eight gallon fuel tank, situated directly in front of the windscreen and the stricken fighter went into a spin. With the engine gone the centre of gravity moved back drastically. To offset the weight shift, Ron Mitchell pushed the control column hard forward and pulled back the cockpit canopy. He would have to get out, for there was little hope of putting the Spitfire down in one piece.

The aircraft was falling rapidly through the clouds and beginning to go into a series of turns. Through the smoke sweeping past the cockpit, Ron could see some houses below—he was above a built-up area. That decided him. He had regained a little control, but was still unable to prevent the turning, so he would stay with it and attempt to put it down where it would do least harm.

An open space, a recreation ground, presented itself. He managed to nudge the spiralling aeroplane towards it.

The next thing he remembered was sitting in the cockpit—all movement had ceased and flames were beginning to break through the instrument panel. Co-ordination between his limbs and his brain did not appear to exist; he couldn't move to undo the harness—he would be cooked where he sat.

Suddenly, strong arms were working around him, unfastening buckles and pulling away straps. Through the heavy smoke he could make out the uniform of a petty officer in the Royal Navy, and the outline of another man. The man, who turned out to be a farm labourer, lifted him bodily from the blazing coffin and carried him to safety. The Spitfire was gutted.

Another fact that he was able to bring back to mind was that the pilot who had rammed him in mid-air, was a trainee fighter pilot from the same unit. Apparently he had made no attempt to leave his aircraft and had been killed.

"What do you remember after that?" prompted Doctor Crichton.

The hospital, his injuries, also his convalescence . . . it all began to come back to him, but nothing at all of the months since that time. He was suffering from a severe case of amnesia after receiving a bang on the head from a second crash, which had left a wrecked Spitfire close to the 'Lord's Seat' on Rushup Edge, Derbyshire.

In addition to the blow on the head, Ron had suffered a fractured arm and leg, plus frostbite. To aid his full recovery, the RAF doctor began to fill in the blanks in the pilot's memory. He was reminded that he had been in a flight of four Spitfires when he had informed his leader that he had run out of fuel. He had then dropped out of formation and simply disappeared.

At Hibalstow, the satellite field for Kirton-in-Lindsey, the flying control liaison officer had made extensive inquiries of all the airfields in the vicinity, without success. The Royal Observer Corps were asked if any of their posts had spotted the errant Spitfire, but they were unable to help. The police, also, were asked if they would make inquiries; squadrons belonging to Number Four Bomber Group were contacted with a view to conducting an airsearch of the desolate Pennine hills. However, at first, bad weather and overcast skies made an initial search from the air impossible.

Flying Officer Hawkins, the flight leader, made a brave attempt to take his Spitfire up and search the ground below the approximate position where Mitchell had dropped from sight, but as they had been off-course at the time, it was difficult to know where to begin. Before he was able to make a start, the weather forced him to return.

During the following day, Saturday, Halifax bombers roared low over the Pennines with many pairs of eyes peering

Ron Mitchell

through the cloud gaps. As the bombers had been stood down from operations because it was a period of full moon, aircraft in plenty were available to join in the search. During the day one bomber crew spotted what appeared to be wreckage, but then lost sight of it in the overcast. However, a fix was obtained and the approximate position passed on to the police, who instigated a search in that area with the help of the Home Guard.

In the grey light of the full moon, the search parties scoured the hills, but at around 2 am, clouds suddenly descended on top of the hills in typical peakland fashion. With the danger of the searchers themselves becoming lost, scouring of the moorland had to be called off for the time being.

As the men were gathering to turn for base, a civilian helper stumbled upon some wreckage. The news was passed to the police, who in turn told the RAF

Mountain Rescue Team, led by 'Doc' Crichton.

Wreckage was widespread; both wings had been ripped off as the fighter bounced across the moor. The engine was located; then, a little further on, the fuselage. The cockpit was empty and the pilot's parachute lay on the seat; at least the pilot hadn't baled out. He had been well enough to unstrap himself and climb out of the wreckage. There were traces of blood, indicating that the pilot had suffered injury. On the port side of the aircraft, just aft of the wireless compartment, a small hinged panel gave access to a first aid kit—it had been opened and the bandages removed. At least the pilot had been fit enough to treat himself, but that had been over thirty-six hours earlier. Injured and alone on the moors in the middle of winter, the pilot didn't stand much chance of survival. Army units were brought in and every inch of the moor was systematically covered, until, on Sunday lunchtime a figure was discovered crouched up in a hollow in the ground.

After forty-eight hours on the moorland the unconscious pilot was carried off and transported to Buxton Cottage Hospital.

It was 12th December, 1943: Ron Mitchell had suffered severe amnesia, as if the period between his first crash, hospitalisation, recovery and return to flying duties, had never happened. In his mind the two accidents had blurred into one. It was only gradually, over many weeks, that his memory began to return. Like pieces in a jigsaw, one bit of information linked to another until finally, with the help of Doc Crichton, he possessed the complete picture.

The four Spitfires, that had set out on that Friday, had been doing a practice reconnaissance down the east coast; there was no gap in the cloud cover. Ron Mitchell was tagging along in his two and a half year old Spitfire Mk V, flying in the number four position. They were flying at 4,000 feet well above the cloud base and travelling at 230 mph. The flight of Spitfires had been in the air for twenty minutes when suddenly, Ron's engine coughed and went into a series of splutters.

immediately, he pushed the fuel gauge button, which incredibly was registering nought. The tanks must not have been filled after the last flight; but the fuel gauge had not indicated empty tanks, so it must have been faulty. He informed Flying Officer Hawkins of his plight as he watched the other three Spitfires pull away from him. Then he quickly informed base and asked for a homing course. He received instructions and turned onto 090, losing height as he did so.

"During my descent I was not unduly perturbed at making a forced landing, as at the briefing that morning I could see that we were intended to fly above cloud over Lincolnshire and, to keep within reason, close to the east coast. The cloud was as low as 1,000 feet and I had every chance of making a safe landing, wheels up if needs be."

There were numerous airfields in Lincolnshire, plus many flat fields, which should have made it easy for him to put down safely. But the truth was that the flight of Spitfires was seventy miles off course, and over the treacherous peaks of Derbyshire.

He could clearly remember entering the cloud, but nothing else after that. The crash, his survival on the moors for two days and nights, plus thirteen days in Buxton Cottage Hospital, remained a complete blank.

In six months he was flying again, having fully recovered from his injuries, and in August 1944 he joined 611 Fighter Squadron, at Bradwell Bay in Essex. That was the summer period of 1944 when Hitler unleashed his flying bombs against southern England. Equipped

Ron Mitchell (*third from right*) with his fellow pilots, all in high spirits.

with Spitfire IXs, 611 Squadron commenced anti-'Diver' operations, chasing the V1s and bringing them down before they reached populated areas.

After a three month period in Scotland at the close of the year, 611 Squadron returned to the south of England to take up a new role—daylight bomber escort duties.

In February, the Squadron was equipped with long range Mustang IVs and in the following month Ron took part in his last engagement with the enemy, thus making RAF history. The very first RAF fighter squadron to meet the Russians in the air over Germany was 611 Squadron.

As the war was drawing to a close, with Hitler's empire being crushed on two fronts, RAF Bomber Command could

once more venture out in daylight raids over the Third Reich. The Luftwaffe was short on fuel and trained pilots, and was unable to make an effective defence of the Fatherland. Allied fighters, with their exceptional long-range capabilities, could operate where and when they liked in the closing months of the most devastating war in human history.

On April 16th, 611 Squadron was detailed to join a Canadian fighter squadron, they were to fly escort to eighteen Lancaster Bombers, that were *enroute* to attack Swinemunde, on the Baltic coast.

Before the operation the fighter pilots received a warning: after the bombers had turned for home, the fighters were instructed to make for Berlin and 'look for trouble': as the eastern front had swept almost to the gates of the German capital, the pilots were told to be on the lookout for Russian fighters. It would appear that the Americans had recently experienced a brush with their eastern comrades and lost a number of their Thunderbolts. It would seem that the American fighters had been mistaken for FW190s.

Ron Mitchel found himself wingman to the group-leader. He was expected to stay close to him if they ran into trouble. As the Lancasters turned for home, the Mustang fighter escort turned south for Berlin. They had lost one of their charges, but not to enemy fighters, it had been hit by anti-aircraft fire. There was nothing they could have done about that.

The Russian Front, now well into Germany, lay below as they sped for Berlin with the pilots scanning the skies.

"Fighters ten o'clock low," came a cool but urgent voice over the air.

Four . . . five . . . six, Ron counted aloud. Four Yaks and two Shturmoviks. He could clearly make out the red stars on their wings. What would happen if they were attacked? None of them fancied the idea of getting into a scrap with the Ruskies. Nor did they fancy being the instigators of an incident that might lead to another war.

Group-Leader Christie's voice came over their radios, "Let's get out of here, we don't want any trouble with this lot!"

As a man the pilots of the two squadrons opened their throttles and left the Soviet fighters standing. The RAF and Soviet Air Force had met up over the German capital and had not fought one another. Many in the German High Command had hoped that once they met up the Allies would fight it out, thus starting a new east-west conflict. Some even entertained hopes of joining in a war against the Russians.

A few minutes after meeting the Russian aircraft high over Berlin, 611's Adjutant, Flying Officer Partridge, called out, "Bandits—ten of them!"

"They'll be Ruskies!" replied Group-Leader Christie, "Keep your eye on them."

"They're Jerries . . . FW190s," came the cool reply. "I can see the crosses!"

Ron Mitchell stayed tucked in close to the Group-Leader, as the two squadrons dived to the attack. He managed to get some shots off in the general direction of one of the German fighters, but could not be sure of hitting it.

Soon ten columns of smoke coming up from the ground marked the outcome. Every one of the German 'planes had been destroyed without loss to the Mustangs. The German pilots must have been made up of inexperienced youths, to have suffered such a defeat. It certainly demonstrated the poor state that the Luftwaffe had deteriorated to by the Spring of 1945.

After the war Ron continued to fly until 'Stand Down' in January 1957, completing his career as a fighter pilot on the first jet fighters, Meteors and Vampires, with 614 Squadron.

He had flown practically every type and mark of Spitfire, from the Battle of Britain type to the Griffon-engined later models. Then the Mustang long distance fighter. He had 'pranged' twice, and on the second occasion left a bit of his Spitfire on the Derbyshire hills.

Halifax HR727, 51 Squadron, returning to Snaith after bombing Frankfurt, crashed at Blackden Edge, 5th October 1943.
Map reference 132878 • Map key number 34

For each RAF aircraft crash in this country a card was prepared outlining the briefest details. That card, Form 1180, Accident Record Card, concerning the crash of Halifax HR727 V for Victor, held at the Air Historical Branch (RAF) Ministry of Defence, dated 5th October, 1943, contained the following brief and concise information:

"Error in captaincy in breaking cloud when uncertain of position. Lack of fuel and faulty navigation. Pilot did not check engineer's statement that there was four hours fuel left. Engineer failed to keep check and failed to warn of impending fuel shortage. Flight engineer chiefly responsible."

The above is the summary of an in-depth inquiry, instigated by the RAF Flight Safety organisation, with the primary aim of avoiding similiar accidents in the future. It was not possible to include a number of contributory factors to the accident on Form 1180. As the full inquiry documents have since been destroyed, some of those now missing factors are included here.

The two surviving crew members of the Halifax bomber were, the bomb-aimer, Sergeant Victor Garland and the rear-gunner Sergeant Jimmy Mack. The conclusions drawn as to what were the contributory factors to the crash were gathered from statements taken from the two survivors. Would either Garland or Mack find themselves in agreement with the official statement to be read on Form 1180? Knowing what happened on that last flight of V for Victor, on that night

79

Sergeant Ernest Fenning, pilot

in October, 1943, throws some light on the tragedy, fifty years after the event.

The flight engineer, Sergeant Lane, died shortly after the Halifax bomber hit the hilltop and consequently his side of the story has never been told. The only existing official document holds him chiefly responsible for the accident. With the help of the two survivors and a former Halifax flight-engineer (Flight Sergeant Frank Newman, who survived being brought down over enemy occupied territory), the events of that fatal flight have been reconstructed to put alongside the official Accident Record Card.

It was at 20 Operational Training Unit, Lossiemouth, that the crew came together, each from his individual training unit. There was the pilot Ernie Fenning, twenty-one years old and recently married. The navigator was Canadian, 'Gil' Fortin, the grandfather of the crew who had reached the ripe old age of twenty-five. Sergeant Victor Garland was the bomb-aimer and came from Aberdeen—a mere lad of eighteen. The wireless operator was another teenager, Sergeant Frank Squibbs, and defending the aircraft from a stern attack was Sergeant Jimmy Mack, who was aged twenty-three years, from near Berwick-upon-Tweed.

At the OTU the crew learned to operate as a team flying Wellingtons, but they were incomplete as a team of five. Later, at 1652 Heavy Conversion Unit, they took on the last two men that would complete the crew, mid-upper gunner Sergeant Short (Shorty) and flight engineer Eric Lane. The latest member was a necessary requirement for crews moving on to four-engined bombers; Sergeant Lane was twenty-one years old and he, like his Skipper Ernie Fenning, had married whilst doing his aircrew training. After completing their training, the new crew was ready to join in the air battles over Europe and received a posting to 51 Squadron, stationed at Snaith in York- shire.

The Squadron's unofficial name was 'Yorks Own Squadron' and the previous year it had been engaged in anti-submarine patrols with Coastal Com-mand; however, now equipped with Halifax IIs it was back to Bomber Command and Number 4 Group.

As the British bomber offensive contin-ued to grow in momentum, towards the autumn of 1943, nightly excursions took in German cities further and further eastwards towards Berlin and included Mannheim, Kassel, Hanover, and what some crews felt was the 'hottest' target of them all—Frankfurt.

The first operation for the new boys at 51 Squadron, was a mine laying operation trip on 3rd September. Their first attack on a German city took place two nights later when around five hundred bombers attacked Mannheim. A thousand acres of the city were devasted;

four railway stations were gutted along with storehouses and sheds. Warehouses in the district around the docks burned on for three days.

On the following night they made their longest flight over enemy territory when they visited Munich, the birthplace of National Socialism; they were nine and a half hours in the air. On the return trip they were forced to land at Hunsden, near London, because of lack of fuel, completing their journey back to Snaith the following morning.

The men of V for Victor, or 'Vicky', as they affectionately named Halifax HR727, were beginning to knit together as a crew, gaining experience as they went on to other targets: Dunlop rubber factory at Montlucon; marshalling yards at Modane on the French-Italian border; Hanover twice and Mannheim again. They took part in the flattening of Bochum's town centre at the end of September, bringing Vicky's crew to the completion of their first month of operations.

On 3rd October they were among the four hundred and sixty-seven Main Force crews that attacked Kassel. Although the Germans had succeeded in decoying the British 'terror bombers' away from the city, one of the largest ammunition depots in Germany was inadvertently hit. The resulting explosion attracted other aircraft and the dump was completely destroyed.

Bomber losses to defending night-fighters, in the last quarter of the year, began to mount again as the Luftwaffe units began to receive new radar equipment to combat tinfoil jamming.

In July, in an attack upon Hamburg, strips of aluminium foil had been dropped in bundles by the raiders, thus blotting out the German radar screens. However, in less than two months, the German scientists had come up with the 'Lichtenstein SN-2', which once again gave the nightfighter crews the means

VIA BARRY BLUNT

Sergeant Eric Lane, engineer

to wreak havoc among the bomber streams. It was against that background that the events of the night of 4th October, 1943, took place.

Earlier that day Eric Lane had swung his legs out of bed and dragged his uniform on over his six foot frame. On his way to the ablutions he checked the sky—would the weather hold? Would they be going that night? He made his way over to the station building and into the crew room to mark that he was present, by placing a tick beside his name. The blackboard did not carry the chalked message 'stand down 'til' which would have meant an evening at the pub or the pictures—so he concluded that something might well be on that night.

Borrowing a bike, he rode round the perimeter track to where the bombers were parked. It was his task to check the aircraft over and report back to the skipper, Ernie Fenning, that everything was OK. A formality in a way, for the ground crews took a real pride in their work and made sure that everything was 'spot on'.

There she stood, £50,000's worth of heavy bomber, painted black on the sides and underneath the wings; the squadron identification letters MH at one side of the RAF roundel and the aircraft's individual indentification letter on the other the letter V.

Eric dismounted and began his routine checks: cowlings, inspection covers etc., all in place and secure. No oil, fuel or hydraulic leaks, tyres and undercarriage legs OK; in fact everything was in order, as he knew that it would be. Hoisting himself through the hatch in the fuselage, Eric wandered down to the tail and back along the whole length of the aircraft, checking pressure gauges and pipes. Everything seemed to be in order —V for Victor was ready to go.

After lunch at the mess, the tannoy announced 'all crews to briefing at 1400 hours'. The crews of each aircraft sat together in the Operations Room, facing a curtained-off map on the wall. There was a suspicion of a 'sticky' trip that night; some speculation was in the air prompted by the type of bombs being loaded into their aircraft at that moment. Not mines, which would have meant a reasonably easy trip to the Baltic to do some 'gardening' (code word for sowing mines in enemy waters) but rather, high explosives and incendiaries, meaning a trip to one of Hitler's cities.

As the commanding officer entered, accompanied by specialist officers, the crews rose and came to attention.

They were told to be seated and all eyes were upon the curtain, as it was being drawn back to reveal a large map of Europe.

"Gentlemen," he announced, "your target for tonight is Frankfurt!"

A thin piece of red tape dog-legged across the map into Germany, ending at an industrial town on the River Main. A barely perceptable groan ran through the assembled crews—it was going to be nasty.

The raid scheduled for October 4th/5th on Frankfurt, was to be a 'maximum effort'. In order to confuse the German defences and draw off the nightfighters a 'spoof' raid was to be made on Ludwigshafen. In the event, that deception proved to be only partially successful.

Various bombing officers covered their own specialist subjects in turn; navigation, bombing, engineering, gunnery, meteorology and intelligence. Duration of the whole trip was estimated at around eight hours. Fighter and anti-aircraft opposition was expected to be heavy. The target city would be marked with flares dropped by the Pathfinder Force.

The Met officer announced the far from cheery news that, the then misty conditions would develop into a 'pea soup' later in the day. The Squadron would have to head north to clear it, pin-point their position at Berwick-Upon-Tweed, before setting course for Germany. He went on to forecast that the base would be clear upon their return. His confident prediction was to be proved totally inaccurate, as Britain began one of its worst nights of the year.

Each member of the crew of V for Victor absorbed all the particulars relevant to his own function. With the briefing over it was time for the knots in the stomach, the pre-operation nerves and the resulting tension. Casualties in Bomber Command were high, and it had been calculated that, over the months, around one in two would not survive.

AM11405

HALIFAX.H.R.727. MODIFIED RUDDER.

Halifax HR727 had been used in rudder experiments before going to 51 Squadron. Jimmy Mack's 'office' from which he escaped with his life can be clealy seen.

K. A. MERRICK

83

What had come to be a tradition followed later that afternoon—the pre-op bacon and eggs. Then it was time for kitting up at the locker room, where personal effects were handed over. The crew members clambered into their flying gear, and after collecting parachutes, testing microphones and headphones in their helmets they got aboard the trucks that would take them to their respective aircraft.

Eric Lane gave V for Victor another once over externally and then had a word with the ground crew, who were there to see them off. He removed the pitot head cover and stuffed it into his uniform blouse. One by one each crew member slung his gear up through the hatch on the port side and jumped up after it.

All round the airfield at Snaith, wireless operators in their Halifax bombers switched on their sets to warm them up. Three hundred miles away in Belgium, German radio-monitoring stations picked up the radio signals and were alerted to a big raid threat. From the monitoring stations information was passed to fighter operation rooms and nightfighters went to 'standby'. Once the final direction of the bomber stream had been determined, the individual twin-engined fighters would be vectored onto the raiders.

Eric Lane plugged in his intercom and awaited Skipper Ernie Fenning's orders to start up. When it came it was a short trip back to the rest position (two couches mid-way between the main wing spars) to pull on the petrol cocks for tanks 1 and 3, in each wing. Then it was back again to the engineer's panel, situated in an area behind the 'main office', or pilot's position. At the Skipper's command Eric pressed the individual starter and booster buttons for each of the four Rolls Royce Merlin engines. Each crew member, in turn, reported to the pilot that their instruments or equipment were working—it was time to move.

A member of the ground staff guided the bomber from dispersal to the perimeter track, where a queue was forming, awaiting take-off.

From his position in the rear turret, Jimmy Mack could see Halifax J for Jig moving up behind him and exchanged a wave with the bomb-aimer, Sergeant Vose. As V for Victor was given the green light, he both felt and heard the concerted roar of all four engines as the Skipper opened the throttles, and the following line of taxiing bombers were left behind as they swept down the runway. It was 5.30 pm and beginning to get dark as the fog closed in.

It was always a tense moment as a heavily loaded bomber passed the point of no return, just prior to the aircraft becoming 'unstuck' from the ground. To lose an engine at that point, would have meant ploughing on into the fields opposite the end of the runway—with full fuel tanks and loaded with high explosives, it was regarded by the crews as a dangerous exercise.

Once off the deck, the flight engineer's job was to make sure that the undercarriage was locked up, and that the flaps isolating cock was off; then he would set the throttles and engine revs for climbing.

Gilbert Fortin, the Canadian navigator, called through his instructions to the Skipper and V for Victor turned onto a course to rendezvous with hundreds of other bombers, including Lancasters and Halifax bombers from other squadrons and groups, over Berwick.

Every crew member settled down to his job, with the Skipper checking with each one of them, to ensure that everything was working.

Lying in his prone position in the nose, bomb-aimer and teenager, Victor Garland, reported to the navigator that they were crossing the English coastline. Once out over the North Sea the mid-upper gunner Sergeant Shorty

Short, along with rear-gunner Jimmy Mack, requested and were given, permission to test fire their machine-guns.

"Navigator to pilot—turn to course 160 degrees."

Meanwhile,the other teenager in the crew, wireless-operator Frank Squibbs, had been listening out at pre-arranged times for broadcasted revised wind changes; and for the dreaded message that the raid had been cancelled. That would have meant that all the effort and tension up to that point had been in vain; that they would be unable to count the flight against the thirty operations, which made up a tour. After each tour of duty a crew could look forward to six months rest from operational flying.

There was to be no recall from the Frankfurt raid.

Every twenty minutes Eric Lane entered the cylinder head temperatures on his log sheet, along with oil pressures. Fuel consumption was his main concern, as he carefully worked out how much petrol was being used. He would switch from one tank to another, taking care not to let an engine cut out through fuel starvation. The latest model Halifax carried six fuel tanks of various size in each wing; the engineer had to juggle with thirteen levers or cocks to sort out the 1,800 gallons. He had to bear in mind that take-off, landing and over-target periods were critical, and he had to arrange things so that, at those times, he was on tanks one and three to the inner and outer engines respectively. That was because they were the largest and closest tanks to the engines, consequently, they were used at take-off, over the target, and landing. The rest of the tanks were used to fill the gaps. Easy, so long as nothing untoward happened to upset the system, such as losing one engine or having a tank holed, then things could get very complicated for the flight-engineer.

VIA BARRY BLUNT
Sergeant Gilbert Fortin, navigator

"Enemy coast ahead—keep your eyes peeled!" came the Skipper's warning to his crew. All light banter on the intercom ceased, it was to be used strictly for business from then on.

Their zigzag path avoided flak concentrated areas of the heavily defended Ruhr Valley. They were on the last leg leading to the target.

Ahead of the main bomber stream, Lancasters of the Pathfinder Force were busy putting down Blind Marker Illuminators, which were falling within three miles of the aiming point. Greater accuracy was achieved when Primary Visual Markers dropped within one and a half miles of the target centre.

At 9.10 pm V for Victor began its approach at 19,000 feet. Ahead of them the crew could see a mass of searchlight beams probing the sky, trying to latch onto the raiders. Bright orange and red bursts of flame approaching their height and flight path, indicated the presence of some accurate gunners on the ground. The bursting anti-aircraft shells seemed to warn against flying straight and level — but there was nothing for it, it was a necessary part of a bombing run. They had never seen so many searchlights.

"Navigator to pilot, fifteen minutes to target!"

The young Scot bomb-aimer, lying prone in the nose, began busying himself with the bomb sight, setting wind, height, speed and sequence in which the bombs were to be dropped.

It was time for Eric Lane to move. Making his way back to the rest position, he plugged in his intercom. "Engineer to pilot . . . I'm changing to tanks one and three, starboard . . . now!"

Ernie Fenning readied himself to throttle back any engine which might cut out, and to compensate for any resulting swing. The port wing tanks switch followed with no trouble.

Eric's next job was to whip out a screwdriver and remove the inspection covers over each bomb release mechanism. In the event of any bomb failing to drop, he would stick his finger through the hole and let it go manually. He had to make sure that they didn't take any 'hang-ups' back with them.

"Pilot to bomb-aimer, beginning the bomb run now . . . she's all yours!"

"Pilot to air-gunners, watch out for fighters!"

The intercom remained switched on and all crew members could hear young Vic Garland's voice, as he relayed his flight corrections to Fenning.

"Keep her steady at that Skipper . . . left a bit . . . steady, steady, right, right, steady, now . . . steady . . ."

The young Scot's breathing between instructions could be plainly heard by each of the crew members, as they sat tense in their positions. After what seemed like an eternity, the cross on the bomb sight moved onto one of the Pathfinder flares burning three miles below, and the eighteen year old pressed the button on the bomb release clenched in his right hand.

"Bombs gone!" He called.

All of them felt the gentle upward swing as one 1,000-pounder, one 500-pounder, twenty-four 30-pounders and five-hundred and forty 4-pound incendiaries fell towards the city below.

"Engineer to pilot, all bombs gone," he reported.

The bomb doors swung up and inwards as Fenning slammed up the bomb-door lever. But the run over target was not yet over.

"Pilot to engineer—standby photo-flash!"

A picture of the results was required and Eric moved over to the flare chute to despatch a most unwelcome passenger. A photo flare igniting in the centre fuselage could cause havoc. It meant flying straight and level thirty seconds longer. The mid-upper gunner, Shorty, was the most relieved of all the crew to know that the photo-flare had been dropped down the flare chute, as he owned the bottom hanging closest to it. They could take evasive action once that, the last act of a bombing run, had been taken care off.

Meanwhile the RAF's spoof raid on Ludwigshafen had not entirely fooled the enemy, consequently, the nightfighters had not been enticed there. Probably for the reason that the marking had been wide of target, plus the lateness of the decoy raid in getting started. The main attack on Frankfurt was well underway and that convinced the defence controllers that it was, in fact, the main target. That fact was plainly obvious to the Messerschmitt 110 pilots and air-gunners as they climbed to the height of the bombers. The fires burning at Frankfurt were plain enough to see.

"Navigator to pilot, turn to course 280 degrees."

They were going home; it was 9.30 pm. Below and behind them the city's railway marshalling yards, station buildings and warehouses were ablaze; a conflagration that was to last for three days.

In the rear turret, crouched behind four Browning machine guns, Jimmy Mack avoided looking at the fires raging beneath so as not to destroy his night vision. Suddenly, Jimmy Mack's turret turned into day . . . he was temporarily blinded as a searchlight beam struck V for Victor. Other beams immediately swung on, to illuminate the bomber that had been caught, and flak began bursting all around.

No need for any fancy stalking for the nightfighter that was closing in fast on V for Victor. The technique in use at that time was for them to pick up a bomber on their new Lichenstein SN-2 radar sets, close in beneath it, and with twin, upward pointing cannons, open fire at close range. The four-engined RAF bombers made excellent targets, with their large wing areas packed with fuel tanks.

The searchlight batteries had coned one of the hated enemy, and the Messerschmitt pilot would take his chances on being hit by the concentrated flak barrage that was creeping across to the bomber.

Shorty, in the mid-upper turret, glimpsed the closing nightfighter at about the same time that 30mm cannon shells slammed into the port inner engine.

"Fighter! Corkscrew port—Go!"

Ernie Fenning pushed the control

Sergeant Victor Garland, bomb-aimer

column forward and opened the throttles wide. V for Victor, with flames streaming from the port inner, powered out of the searchlight's glare and under the attacking fighter. Part way through the dive Fenning swung the bomber violently to starboard. Each crew member was pressed against the fuselage, their ears popping as the air pressure changed rapidly. They were moving at three hundred miles per hour when Fenning pulled back, taking Vicky into short climb whilst still in the starboard turn; then he went into a further dive. It was a manoeuvre, that when executed at night, was nigh on impossible for any fighter pilot to latch onto and effectively follow.

After corkscrewing down to 9,000 feet,

they could see no sign of their attacker and the engine fire was out. With the damaged engine stopped dead, Fenning quickly feathered the propeller and trimmed the aircraft for straight and level flight.

That little incident would play the devil with Eric Lane's calculations. His first action was to switch-off port number 1 tank. Back at his panel he scanned the petrol gauges and fuel pressure warning lights for the three good engines. As he watched, the needle on the gauge for number 2 tank started to creep back steadily. Quickly, he made his way back to the petrol cocks and plugged in the intercom.

"Engineer to pilot, number 2 tank holed with 64 gallons in—a third of our emergency reserve. Can I run all three engines from it to minimise loss?"

"Pilot to engineer, go ahead . . . it's no use letting it go to waste." Fenning readied himself to throttle back on any engine that might fail through fuel starvation.

With every move that he made, Eric Lane carried on a running commentary over the intercom. "Turning off number 3 . . . now! Turning on number 2, wing balance . . . open."

Suppose the pipes leading to the port outer engine had been fractured? Eric Lane had to take that possibility into account. He peered hard at the warning light to the port outer—not a flicker, it was OK.

"Port outer OK Skipper. Get ready for transfer to starboard!"

A locking wire trapped the transfer cock that would permit fuel to be transferred from one wing to the other. He kept up his vital commentary. If the flight engineer got it right, then there would be no fuel starvation to the two Merlins thundering away on the starboard wing.

"Cutting wire, Skipper, main balance on!"

He watched for a flicker on the starboard inner warning light—all was well. The delicate operation had been completed without mishap. All three engines were pulling from the holed number 2 tank on the port wing. Unpluging his intercom, Eric Lane moved back to his instrument panel and began checking each dial. He was relieved to note, that the three engines were obviously undamaged and running sweet; and that the other fuel tanks seemed sound. They had got off lightly, but he would have to concentrate on that number 2 gauge, which at that point was indicating around fifty-five gallons—the leak wasn't massive.

The rest of the crew were able to report that they were unhurt, and that both their instruments and equipment were functioning satisfactorily.

Eric Lane performed his next duty: taking a torch he began checking through the aircraft for holes and sparks coming from damaged electrics, also that reservoir pressures were normal. Again he was able to report to Ernie Fenning that everything appeared to be OK.

A further one hundred and fifty miles on the homeward leg, a further course change was made, and the limping Halifax turned onto a north-westerly heading.

From his position in the tail, Jimmy Mack could see, even at that distance, the glow of fires as Frankfurt burned. Both he and the mid-upper gunner, Shorty, were told by Fenning to keep an extra lookout for nightfighters, as they were well below the main bomber stream and alone.

Back in the engineer's position, Eric Lane began his calculations. They were vital for their safe return to Snaith. He dare not allow the damaged number 2 tank fall below twenty gallons and run the risk of three engines cutting out together. He totalled up the fuel in the good tanks, then read off the engine revs, boost and altitude. From that, he worked out the fuel consumption, divided one from the other and the figure that he was left with gave him the total flying time available to them.

"Engineer to pilot, four hours flying time left."

Gil Fortin, the Canadian navigator, using the flight engineer's calculations was able to give the estimated time of arrival—at around 1.15 am they would be home—that was if the forecasted winds hadn't changed.

"Pilot to engineer, can you give me a rundown on the accessories we have lost?"

That was yet another problem for Eric Lane to consider. Each of the four engines drove generators and, or, pumps, which performed various functions throughout the aircraft. Lose an engine and you lost certain services along with it. He began making a list of services that they would no longer be able to call upon, because the port inner engine had stopped turning. Wheel brakes, automatic pilot, undercarriage flaps, radiator shutters. Important functions that they would have to operate manually by emergency means. Electrically, the generator on the port inner also packed juice into a 24 volt accumulator, which in turn provided power to operate the mid-upper gun turret and, more importantly, the beam approach equipment and radio.

With number 2 gauge indicating just twenty gallons, Eric Lane began to juggle with the petrol cocks, to get back to the comparative safety of one tank, one engine. There was equal fuel in each wing, but the starboard side was being used at twice the rate, so unless he could balance the position, they could well end up with empty tanks on one side, a heavy load on the other and only one engine to bear it. Both he and the Skipper were confident that they could cope with the problem.

V for Victor crossed the enemy coast and was soon over the Channel.

Sergeant James Mack, rear-gunner

"Bomb-aimer to navigator, we're over Beachy Head!"

They were on course and heading for their beds in Yorkshire, another op under their belts. The limping bomber droned northwards towards a heavy weather front that was moving across central and northern England.

"Wireless-operator to pilot, bad reception Skipper . . . I can't pick up the met. reports."

The fact was, young Squibbs the eighteen year old 'sparks', was operating a dying set, as power in the accumulator was being used up. With the help of the navigator, he let out a trailing aerial to try to improve reception. With the bad weather and the fuel situation, it was no time for the aircraft to go deaf with radio failure. They needed those revised weather reports every half hour.

"Bomb-aimer to navigator, we're over Reading."

A little further north, as the bomber entered the bad weather front, the radio gave up completely. No more help for the navigator, no radio direction finding aid, no broadcast revised winds, no emergency calls on 'Darkie' to anyone on the ground. They were rendered speechless and deaf. They were also blind, they could see no landmarks, as rain lashed the limping aircraft.

"Navigator to pilot, we're port of track, that is, if the winds haven't changed. We should be over the base in fifteen minutes."

Skipper Ernie Fenning had to make some decisions and make them fast. He knew that he couldn't hang about in the clouds. The fuel situation was becoming critical and he would need time over the 'drome to determine the serviceability of the undercarriage. If it had been damaged in the nightfighter attack, then they would have to divert to a grass, emergency landing strip, and time was rapidly running out. The altimeter was showing around 2,000 feet and they were still in cloud. If they could get below it they could 'pundit' crawl home. They had successfully used that method in the past, sighting the marker beacons flashed by individual airfields and plotting their flight path to the next one.

Vic Garland, the bomb-aimer, left his position in the nose, where he had been looking out for landmarks, and went to stand in the second pilot's position. He was there to look out for flashing beacon lights and point them out to Ernie Fenning, once they had dropped below cloud.

"Engineer to pilot . . . we're almost out of fuel Skipper." Eric Lane was expecting that at any moment his three faithful Merlins would splutter to a stop.

"Pilot to crew, watch your ears, we're going down!"

V for Victor never went into that descent. Vic Garland recalled what happened as Fenning stopped speaking:

"Suddenly, I felt that I was in a small room, about five feet wide, getting thrown from one wall to another. When I came to, I was lying on the ground with parts of the cockpit surrounding me. I tried to stand up, but found that my ankles were broken."

In the rear turret, Jimmy Mack thought that they must have collided with another aircraft. He remembered being banged about in his small confined space and ending up lying on the moorland. As he lay there, looking up into the swirling blackness of the night, it all seemed ominously quiet and strange. Having had the vibration and roar of Merlin engines for the past eight hours, it was suddenly quite peaceful.

Jimmy's limbs seemed to all be in order and he found that he was able to stand, but where was the remainder of the aircraft? He could make out the shattered remains of his turret, and some tail section, but the remainder of the aircraft, fragmented and broken, spilled off into the darkness.

The sound of a whistle broke the silence. Someone else was alive out there in the darkness of the moorland. Jimmy Mack took his own whistle, which was attached to his battledress blouse collar, and gave an answering blast. Moving off in the direction of the whistle, Jimmy stumbled upon Eric Lane.

"I'm hurt bad Jimmy," Eric gasped. He appeared to be in a great deal of pain, but Jimmy could find no sign of injury, no marks.

Fifteen feet further along, lying amidst the shattered wreckage of the cockpit,

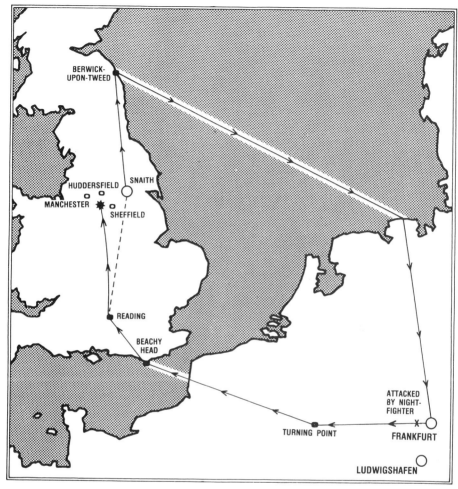

Jimmy Mack came upon Vic Garland. "It's my ankles, they're in a mess, but otherwise I'm not too bad. You'd better check on the others."

Not too far away from him was the Skipper, Ernie Fenning; he had died instantly. Hunting around the wreckage he came upon the bodies of Short, Fortin and the young teenage wireless operator Frank Squibbs—there was nothing he could do for them.

"I'm going for help," Jimmy informed the other two survivors as he set about doing what he could to make them comfortable.

"Don't leave me Jimmy," groaned the flight engineer. "I'm dying."

"You'll be allright, Eric, Vic Garland is in a worse state than you. There's not a mark on you." So saying, the rear-gunner began his descent off Blackden Edge, in Derbyshire, where Halifax V for Victor had so suddenly and tragically come to rest. They had been a few minutes flying time from Snaith, but, with no flying aids, appalling weather and the Pennine mountains in the way, it had made little difference.

The crash had taken place between one and one thirty in the morning. It was

91

At the crash site some substantial pieces of wreckage remain—an inspection cover with the words 'OIL X/X' stencilled on it, and a large sheet of armour plate.

around noon when the rescue services at last located. Eric Lane had died during that time, his injuries being of a massive internal kind. Both Garland and Jimmy Mack were taken to Sheffield Infirmary, then transferred to an RAF hospital. After four months, Vic Garland moved to an aircrew convalescent home at Hoylake in Cheshire. After three months there he was posted as an instructor to a HCU (heavy conversion unit). From there, Vic Garland joined another aircrew and flew a further twenty-six bomber operations with 51 Squadron. The injuries to both his ankles did not prevent him from playing for Scotland at lawn tennis and table tennis, after the war. He went on to work as a senior technical representative with a large paper mill.

Jimmy Mack joined another crew pending a medical to see if he was fit for flying on operations. He was taken off on medical grounds. then on the very first operation, the crew that he had been assigned to, failed to return. He went on to serve as butler and valet to Sir Ralph Carr-Ellison, TD, DL, at Hedgeley Hall, Northumberland.

Who was responsible for the crash of V for Victor? The Accident Record Card at the Ministry of Defence, which is a summary of the in-depth proceedings of an inquiry carried out at the time, states: 'Flight-engineer chiefly responsible'. There is no room to mention the loss of one engine and the resulting loss of other essential functions, and along with that, the complicated juggling act with fuel tanks. No mention of the appalling weather conditions on the approaches to Snaith; stress and fatigue are not recorded on Form 1180. It's little wonder that Eric Lane failed to fill in his log on that return trip, as we have seen from this reconstruction, he was fully employed. Where then did the fault and the responsibility lie for the crash of Halifax HR727 and the loss of four men?

A piece of armour plate.
A castle nut with locking wire.

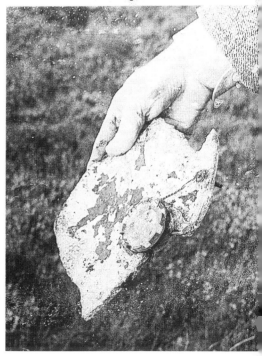

Consider, teenagers and young men in their early twenties, formed into teams and given charge of complex flying machines after a minimum of training; then sent off in the night on round trips of upwards of a thousand miles, carrying high explosives and incendiaries to drop on German civilians. Eight hours in the air, hounded by anti-aircraft fire, searchlights and nightfighters; in danger from mid-air collisions and from being struck by bombs falling from friendly bombers above. Dogged by equipment failures and atrocious weather conditions. Those were all factors which had to be handled three or four times a week. So it went on month after month until chance and cold statistics caught up with the crew and scrubbed them from the active service list, and placed them on the memorial rolls.

Who was responsible for the crash? Perhaps blame could be laid with the nightfighter crew, who scored a direct hit on V for Victor's port inner engine over Frankfurt.

Halifax crash site. MIKE LAWTON

Stirling LJ628, 1654 Heavy Conversion Unit, Wigsley, practising two and three engine flying, crashed on Upper Commons, 21st July, 1944.
Map reference 202957 ● Map key number 35

It was a far cry from the Wimpys that they had been trained on, at 29 Operational Training Unit, Sergeant Coulson decided as he gazed up at the Stirling bomber towering above him.

He had been selected and trained as a bomb-aimer, and had become part of a crew at 29 OTU, Bruntingthorpe near Lutterworth, Leicestershire. For the final part of their training, they had been posted to 1654 Heavy Conversion Unit at Wigsley and Swinderby, near Lincoln.

It was July, 1944, the invasion of Europe had taken place the previous month and the RAF bomber offensive had reached a peak. Losses were heavy among the bomber crews, consequently, each of the HCUs were busy supplying replacement crews to operational squadrons, at the rate of thirty to thirty-five a month.

The principal four-engined, training aircraft in use at the HCUs was the Short Stirling. First of the RAF 'heavies', the Stirling had been gradually relegated to training roles because of operational shortcomings.

The wings were short, Jim Coulson observed, making the fuselage seem disproportionately long. Not the fault of the designers at Short Brothers, who had faithfully created the Stirling to an Air Ministry specification. Standard RAF aircraft hangar doors were one hundred feet wide, so it had been carefully specified that the four-engined bomber should have a wing span less than that. With that restriction, the resultant aircraft was unable to fly at any great height. As enemy defensive ground fire improved, the Stirling became an easy target, as it flew over the area to be bombed at a mere 12,000 feet. The designers had been forced, by the laws of aerodynamics, to place their short-length wings mid-way up the fuselage. In turn, that meant installing an extra large undercarriage which would angle the aircraft sufficiently to ensure lift-off from the ground.

Jim Coulson was six feet tall, and yet he could barely peer over the tyres of the massive wheels of the mighty giant.

95

Sergeant James Coulson, bomb-aimer

numerous accidents as heavily laden bombers had left runways and careered across airfields. Apparently, that tendency was far from slight when the Stirling was in the hands of a novice pilot.

It was to be a full aircraft that morning for the crew's first flight. There were the six original crew members who had come togther at 29 OTU. Pilot, Flying Officer Gardiner; navigator, Sergeant McDonald from Inverness; bomb-aimer, Sergeant Jim Coulson; wireless operator, Sergeant 'Tex' Burroughs, a fellow Londoner; rear-gunner, Sergeant Lennox 'Swig' van Nierkirk and mid-upper gunner Sergeant 'Bunny' Austin, both from Rhodesia.

With conversion to four engines, a flight-engineer had joined the crew; it was his first flight with his new crew and first time in a Stirling. Showing him the 'ropes' was flight engineer, Sergeant John Gittings, who was 'resting' between operations with 467 Squadron.

Sitting in the second pilot's seat, as flying instructor, was Flying Officer O'Leary. Quite a crowd, but then to top it all, a squadron leader elected to fly with them. Ten men in total in Stirling Mark III, LJ628.

There was constant flow of intercom chatter between pilot and engineer prior to actual take-off. Jim Coulson, as bomb-aimer, took no part in the proceedings — he was along for the ride. He moved back from the nose, which seemed a heck of a long way from the ground, ready for take-off.

Under the watchful eye of the pilot instructor, Gardiner opened the throttles gradually until all four engines were running at 2,000 revolutions per minute. He then released the brakes and the bomber began to move steadily forward. The expected swing to starboard came early, but he was ready and smoothly counteracted it. He eased the control column forward and the huge tail came up off the ground and with the runway being eaten up at an ever-increasing rate,

It would be the Skipper's job to learn to handle the Bristol Hercules engines in the next few weeks, but to the young Londoner, it seemed that their pilot's work would be cut out just mastering take-off and landing the Stirling.

Flying Officer Gardiner, prior to his first ever flight in the Stirling scheduled for that morning, had read and re-read the pilot's manual. Under the section headed, 'Take-off', he had noted a cautionary warning: 'Open the throttles slowly (holding all four levers with one hand) the starboard throttles leading, to counteract the slight tendency to swing to starboard'.

As pilot and skipper he had been warned that the Stirling tended, on take-off, to veer to the right resulting in

he pulled back and the metal giant, travelling at 110mph, became airborne.

Once the enormous undercarriage had been retracted, Jim Coulson moved back into the nose and began to familiarise himself with the layout. At least, he decided, he had much more room than he had hitherto enjoyed, lying prone in the nose of the Wellington.

It was 10.05am as Stirling LJ628 lifted from the runway at Wigsley and climbed above the clouds.

Once they had reached 10,000 feet, Gardiner was given the feel of flying a four-engined bomber, first with one engine stopped, and then another. They knew that they were over the flat countryside of Lincolnshire and began to execute a rated descent into the cloud cover with one engine stopped. They had been flying for about twenty minutes.

In the nose, Jim Coulson busied himself checking for leaks. He swung himself up into the front turret and began to explore the unfamiliar surroundings. Cloud swirled about the perspex as he took out his little black book and began to make an entry. Glancing up he could hardly believe his eyes, and he yelled into the intercom:

"Pull up! Pull the flaming nose up Skipper!"

Ground was flashing past a few feet beneath the aircraft.

Gardiner's reaction was immediate — he pulled hard back on the control column and the Stirling reared up and 'bellied' on the moor. They were forty-five miles east of where they thought they were.

The initial impact bounced the rear turret off the 'plane, complete with Swig van Nierkirk still in it. Tail and both wings were ripped off as the giant bomber bumped and slewed across Upper Commons, Bradfield, near Sheffield.

Three escape hatches along the fuselage were thrown open and six men scrambled out bruised and shaken. The two flight engineers were able to

Sergeant John Gittings, engineer

scramble out through the open end of the broken fuselage.

The squadron leader took a quick check and discovered that two of the crew were unaccounted for. One look at the smashed up and squashed bomb-aimer's position, and they feared the worst for Jim Coulson. A groan was heard coming from the twisted gun-turret, however, access to the turret was completely cut off from inside. An axe stowed behind the pilot's seat was brought out and the ones least shaken began chopping at the thin metal skin. There was little danger of fire breaking out and threatening the trapped bomb-aimer; the wings containing the fuel tanks had been ripped away from the fuselage.

After fifteen minutes of chopping, Jim

Coulson was eased out of the nose-turret through the jagged opening. A parachute was opened up and, after injuries to his head and one arm were dressed, he was wrapped in it.

Flight engineer, instructor, Sergeant John Gittings recalled the events of that morning:

"I was standing up looking out of the astrodome, facing the rear of the aircraft. The cloud was very dense, but I did think that I glimpsed a lake below through an odd break in the cloud.

"We began to descend through the cloud, one minute we were flying, the next I was flung six feet to eight feet up the fuselage and ended up sprawled over the other flight engineer. The aircraft was slithering and bumping across the ground.

"Once we had come to a stop the flight engineer expressed his concern for the rear-gunner. We could see daylight where the fuselage had broken in half and scrambled through the break and onto the moorland. We ran towards the tail section, only to discover that the gun turret was missing. It had bounced off on first impact and lay further down the moor. When we reached it we discovered it was empty. In the meantime, some of the others had located the rear-gunner, Swig van Nierkirk, lying under the broken tail — we had run right past him.

"No one had the slightest idea where we were. Two of the crew were given a compass and sent off to get help. As no help had arrived by 2pm, Squadron Leader Hadland, and another crew member, set out to find a way off the desolate moorland.

"Six hours after we had crashed, help arrived in the shape of the chief flying instructor from Wigsley, Squadron Leader Petty along with two army chaps carrying stretchers. guided by two members of the crew.

"We all left the aircraft and walked, taking it in turns to carry the two stretchers. After about an hour we reached the road, and from there the wounded were taken to hospital. The rest of us stayed in an army camp for the night.

"Next morning we were picked up by a lorry and taken back to Wigsley, calling on the way at Sheffield to see how Coulson and Nierkirk were."

The two injured men were taken to Wharncliffe Hospital by members of an RAMC unit, where they both underwent operations.

First to make a full recovery was the Rhodesian rear-gunner, Swig, who was able to rejoin the crew, and along with them was posted to 44 Squadron. They went on to complete a tour of operations and survived the war.

After six weeks, Jim Coulson went on to the Lancaster Finishing School at Syerston and to another crew. He was welcomed at the LFS by his new skipper, a Canadian-Chinese, Flying Officer A E Jung. With his new crew Jim completed a tour with 50 Squadron, flying Lancasters. He never again set foot in a Stirling bomber—his trip on that morning on the 21st July, 1944, had been his first and last flight on that historic aircraft type.

In 1951 he went to live in Canada with his wife Anne, an ex-photographer in the WAAF. Jim Coulson died on 25th March, 1979.

Tex Burroughs, who lives in New Zealand, recalled the events surrounding the accident:

"I don't know any of the details leading up to the crash, because I was on the radio the majority of the time, only coming onto the intercom to give weather reports, or the results of check broadcasts. What is still very clear in my mind, is looking out of my window and thinking how close the ground had become. Before I could make any comment on that to the Skipper, or pass any weather info, we had hit.

"I remember bracing myself with my hands pressed against my work desk, and pushing back into my very efficient and well-upholstered chair. That was a first class piece of furniture; I am sure that it helped in a big way to keep me from serious injury. There followed an awful screeching and screaming of heavily tortured metal, associated with lots of ups and downs, until one violent movement flung me sideways out of my seat and into an electrical panel. I slithered down it and sat, in somewhat of a dazed heap, on the floor. Someone shouted a warning, the full text of which I have forgotten, but I do remember that it contained the word 'fire!'

"In the next instant I was up and out of that aircraft so fast. In retrospect, that is where my training came to the fore because, to this day I do not remember having to duck under the oxygen bottles, which were secured in a circular arrangement over the main spar; or for that matter, having to negotiate the main spar in my dash to evacuate by the rear door. I just went straight down the fuselage and out—but not by the rear door! Instead I went out through a hole left by a departed rear turret. We discovered it several yards from where the aircraft had finally come to rest. The rear-gunner, a young lad called Lennox van Nierkirk, was knocked out cold. Van Nierkirk was from Que-que, in Rhodesia.

"The bomb-aimer was retrieved from amongst the heather, mud and what remained of the bomb-aimer's compartment in the nose section, he apparently having been there at the time looking, so I heard, for a landmark.

"His name was James Coulson and he came from Hackney, London. He never caught up with the crew again after that. Both those boys were covered in parachutes to keep them warm, given first aid and placed under what remained of the port wing. A further 'chute was rigged to keep the cold out, and we tried

Sergeant 'Tex' Burrows, wireless operator

to make them as comfortable as possible.

"Two of the crew, I believe that it was my Captain, Flight Lieutenant Gardiner along with the commander of B Flight, a squadron leader, whose name I can't recall, took off across the moors to get help. In the meantime, in addition to trying to keep up the spirits of the injured, I tried my radio and found that the receiver still worked. In spite of my efforts though, I could not get the transmitter to function.

"Then I thought of the dinghy radio — here was a chance for me to try it out for real. So out it came and up went the kite; there was plenty of wind, and then I spent some time grinding away at the handle, sending out an automatic distress signal. Whether anyone received it, and what action was taken if they did, I never found out. Its range would have been pretty limited in that sort of terrain. But whoever it was that encouraged me in my efforts must have thought that it would at least keep me occupied.

"After what appeared to be a considerable lapse of time, help arrived in the form of uniformed men, with a couple of stretchers. We placed the two injured crew members on them and trekked off across the moorland, back in the direction from which the help had come. Carrying those guys across the ups and downs, across the gullies, through heather and gorse, to the road and the waiting transport, seemed endless. If someone now said that it was X number of miles that we covered, I would not argue. It sure seemed like a long way.

"I remember going along with the two injured in an ambulance to Wharncliffe Emergency Hospital outside of Sheffield. I can recall going there very well for there was a queue of ambulances waiting outside to disgorge their wounded occupants. I was told that the battle for Caen, in northern France was at its height. We had a little wait before we could get unloaded and looked after. They

A complete radiator showing little signs of crash damage.

gave me a bed for the night and I found myself next to some poor soldier boy who had copped a packet from a phosphorus bomb. Nevertheless, he was cheerful in spite of looking like the invisible man in all his bandages. He must have been in great pain.

"A funny thing happened to me whilst I was there. I had been to have a bath and was on my way back to the ward, when I took a wrong turning and finished up in a ward choc-a-bloc with Jerry

Stirling crash site on Upper Commons where large amounts of wreckage may still be seen.

wounded. So there I was, confronted by the enemy, face to face, for the very first time. It was a strange experience and, making a quick recovery, I about-turned 180 degrees and got out quickly. The rest of the crew, so I was told, spent that night being entertained in an army rest camp. I don't recall being transported back to our base, or what transpired when we got back. I know that the wireless operators were pleased to see me alive.

"I remember being sent on survival leave, and how pleased my family was to discover that I was still alive and kicking; they had been sent a telegram to say that I had been involved in an aircrash, and nothing else.

"Things are pretty vague after that, I cannot recall if there was an investigation, and if there was, whether or not I was involved."

The crew, with the exception of the bomb-aimer, stayed together and went on to complete a tour of operations flying Avro Lancasters with 44 (Rhodesian) Squadron.

Mr Gittings, ex-engineer, returned to the crash site in September 1981. Here he is pictured with one of the undercarriage legs, which is still complete with tyre and inner tube.

Anson N9853, 16 Service Flying Training School, Newton, flying to Millom, crashed on Edale Moor, 11th December, 1944.

Map reference 101878 ● Map key number 36

It was to the sizeable contingent of Polish Army and Air Force personnel who found their way to the west, that Hitler gave the nickname 'Sikorski's Tourists'. Defeated when their country was invaded from the west by Germany and from the east by Russia, thousands of Poles reached French soil by devious routes to continue the fight. Then, with the collapse of France, the Poles, as units and as individuals, departed for England, where they were to become an effective force in the Allied war effort.

Each Pole who made it to the British Isles had a story to tell — his personal experiences of escape, evasion and continued fight against Nazi Germany. On 11th December, 1944, an Avro Anson carrying five of Sikorski's Tourists crashed at Edale, injuring two of them.

One of the injured was Jan Klimczak, who was the station's electrical engineer with 16 Service Flying Training School at Newton, in Nottinghamshire.

The purpose of the trip that morning was to take three flying instructors to Millom, in Cumbria. Flying Officer Jan Klimczak was going along to inspect some new American electrical and navigational equipment. Operating the wire-

Flight Lieutenant Witold Suida

less was Flight Sergeant Pasinski.

Adverse weather conditions had restricted flying during the first few days of December, but conditions had improved on the morning of the 11th.

By 9.30 am they were airborne and heading north. Klimczak was in the front seat next to the pilot. None of them bothered to strap himself in — after all, it was just a routine flight, a 130-mile trip. As they approached the Pennines, the clouds closed in and snow swirled about the old 'station bus', as the Anson was affectionately known.

The pilot, Chelstowski, decided to drop through the clouds so as to check his position. It appeared a safe enough manoeuvre, as the altimeter was showing a healthy 2,500 feet of space beneath them.

Jan Klimczak peered up at what seemed to be a cockpit light, and wondered who had put it there. He made a mental note to rebuke someone for it when they got back — it was a stupid place to install a light, and unnecessary.

Someone was crying out in pain, and that noise seemed to have taken the place of the noise of the roar of the two Cheetah engines. He decided that he would go back to sleep again . . .

What he didn't realise was that they were no longer in the air. Shortly before 10am Anson N9853 had descended through cloud and slammed into Edale Moor. The aircraft lay upon its back; the light that the dazed electrical engineer had noted was not in the roof, nor was it a light — it was a hole in the floor of the Anson.

He had been rolled up into a ball by the impact, breaking both arms and a leg. The pilot, Chelstowski, was being pulled through the windscreen when Klimczak again regained consciousness. Two of the passengers, Melcinski and Flight Lieutenant Suida, had escaped serious injury and were able to minister to the others.

An attempt was made to extract Klimczak from the wreckage, through the side of the broken fuselage, but it was too difficult a job — it would take axes to cut him free. Melcinski and Suida opened parachutes and wrapped them around their injured comrades.

It was Melcinski who went for help — walking down from Upper Tor to Edale. At around 2pm that afternoon, a rescue party from the local village arrived at the scene and firemen cut Klimczak free from the wreckage. The wireless operator, Pasinski, was in a great deal of pain as he had suffered injuries to his liver. He and Klimczak were the most seriously injured. From the crash site they were taken to the hospital at RAF Wilmslow, where Jan lay unconscious for eleven days. There was a big gap in his right leg which required four inches of hip bone to be grafted in. After twenty-two months of recuperation he was posted to 3 FTS at Feltwell for electrical duties. Because of the shortage of electrical engineers, Jan Klimczak, despite his injuries, served for another two years. He was granted an 80 per cent disability retirement from the RAF and settled at Collingham, near Newark. He married a WAAF girl whom he met while serving at Newton, and opened an electrical business.

All six Polish airmen who were involved in the crash at Edale survived the war. The pilot, Flight Lieutenant Chelstowski, received the blame for the accident. It was considered by the investigating officers that there had been negligence on his part, and his pilot's log book was endorsed with the words 'gross carelessness'.

Jan Klimczak, however, does not blame the pilot, but rather the altimeter, which was an old Mk1 type, and permitted a 500-foot error. That amount of error was unacceptable when flying over hills enveloped in clouds... a regular feature of the Peak District.

It wasn't the first time that Jan Klimczak had been involved in an aeroplane crash and had ended upside-down.

When he was twenty-one years old he had served as a reservist in the Polish Air Force and was based at a place called Puck, on the Baltic coast. Jan had been ordered by the station commanding officer to go along with him as 'ballast' in a two-seater biplane — a French Potez 25. As they were coming in to land on the short-length field, the tailplane struck a high banking, which flipped the biplane over and they landed upside-down. They hung from their seat straps with aviation fuel soaking them from the ruptured tank. Klimczak was able to free himself and to rescue his commanding officer, who was entangled in his harness and was terrified of being burned alive should the fuel ignite.

On that occasion there were no injuries. Nine years later Jan would flee his homeland, never to return. Within a few weeks of the German invasion of Poland, the young electrical engineer would

Flying Officer Jan Klimczak

begin a 5,000-mile journey, starting from a secret airfield at Wielicko in eastern Poland, and ending in Liverpool, England.

Early in the morning of 1st September, 1939, on two sections of a 1,750-mile frontier with Poland, the Germans launched their attack. At great speed their mechanised columns overtook the Polish Army units that were falling back to man rearward positions. The Polish Army was being sliced up into unco-ordinated units by the enveloping actions of the Panzer divisions.

On 3rd September, Britain and France declared war on Germany.

One of the Cheetah engines with two of its cylinders missing—removed by souvenir hunters.

Some wood and metal scraps litter a gully on Edale Moor *MIKE LAWTON*

Jan was on his annual holiday in August 1939, and returned home at the end of the month to find that he was a wanted man! The police had been searching for him since the 21st, with his mobilisation papers — he was a reservist. Immediately he reported to his unit, the 27th Technical Unit of the First Air Regiment, stationed temporarily on the racecourse in Warsaw.

By then, military units, if they could, were escaping to the east, where they were hoping to regroup. On 2nd September, 27th Technical Unit moved all their equipment to the marshalling yards of Warsaw Central Station. Loaded up onto cattle trucks, men and equipment, they too moved off eastward. It was a slow journey as the lines were in demand for other military traffic. That night they reached a town called Kowell, where they left the railway and continued in trucks to a secret air base at Wielicko, 20 miles south of the town.

As he surveyed the huge country estate there was nothing to indicate the presence of bomber aircraft; no runways, just open, flat fields skirted by woods. Beneath the trees were twin-engined PZL P37 Los bombers. It was a small, fast aircraft, yet able to deliver 5,688 pounds of explosives. The Polish Air Force did not possess enough of them to hinder the invaders seriously. At that point in time, Jan Klimczak was unaware of the shortage in modern equipment.

There were no tents and that night he slept out under the stars with the other hundred-plus men of his unit. In the days that followed, the airfield was prepared for operations. Fuel arrived by horse-drawn waggons and bombs turned up on buses that had been commandeered in the emergency.

A Polish airfield prior to the German and Soviet invasion. In the foreground are the ground crew and air crew of a PZL P37 LOSB bomber. In the background are obsolete Polish fighters (PZL P11Cs).

With the main Polish forces cut off by the pincer movements of the Blitzkrieg, the Polish Commander-in-Chief, Marshal Rydz-Smigly, ordered a general retreat into south-east Poland. A week later all operations ceased at the secret airfield and 27th Technical Unit was ordered to drive to the Romanian border. Thirty lorries with equipment and portable workshops moved out from Wielicko. Whilst on the road the column was attacked from the air three times, as they pushed on day and night along tracks packed with refugees and miscellaneous military units.

On 17th September, forces of the Soviet Union advanced into Poland from the east. It was signalled to fleeing personnel of 27th Technical Unit when an aircraft flew low overhead with the red stars of the Soviet Air Force on the wings and fuselage. They knew then that all was lost.

The column turned away from the Red invasion and headed for Hungary. With Russian tanks just five miles away, they crossed the border at Jasenie. With the unit still intact and the whole column in order, the 27th drove into Monkachevo, where they handed over their arms and equipment to the Hungarian military authority. According to international law they were interned and were housed in a chicory factory at Nagy-Kanizsa, 125 miles from the capital, Budapest.

They would have to escape, Jan Klimczak decided. As they had passed through the main railway station in the capital, a woman had slipped a card with an address on it to one of the men from the unit.

Also in the internment camp was a postman who had escaped by walking from Poland to Hungary, but his postman's uniform would attract less attention than that of a Polish airman. Jan asked him to swap and an exchange was agreed to; the postman's shoes were

108

worn out and the coat and trousers were in a poor state. Two others managed to arrange an exchange for civilian clothes and they joined Klimczak.

They broke out of the internment camp and caught a train to Budapest where, late at night, they arrived at the address they had been given. Fearing some sort of trap, the three Poles hid in the bushes and watched the house for a time. Eventually, a car drew up outside the house and the mysterious woman stepped out, accompanied by a Hungarian army officer.

The three could hear them talking and were surprised to find that they where speaking in Polish. That decided them, they would risk it; they approached the couple and proferred the card that the mystery woman had handed out to their unit at the station. The Hungarian officer, at that point, discreetly took his leave. Jan Klimczak recalled what happened next:

"Her flat was already filled with fleeing Poles, so we stayed the night with the chauffeur. Next day she fitted me up with one of her husband's suits; it was

On the run and arriving in Athens. Klimczak is on the right in his borrowed suit.

of good quality, for her husband was a professor at Budapest University."

The next day they were taken to the Polish Consulate, where they easily avoided the guards that the Hungarians had placed on the door. Once inside the building they were issued with passports and money. Visas were attached to the passports that would take them to England.

They were put on a train that took

Klimczak and his fellow escapees arrive in France and are incorporated into the French air force. Here they are seen examining a Potez 63, a light bomber of the Armee de l'Air.

When the Poles began arriving in France they were sorted and formed into units of the Armee de l'Air, Klimczak is in the first row standing, seventh from the left.

them to Belgrade in Yugoslavia. They made straight for the Polish Consulate, where they were given money and train tickets to Athens. An efficient system seemed to have been hurriedly established which processed and progressed escaping Polish military personnel through south-eastern Europe, across the Mediterranean into France, where they could be re-formed into units to take up the fight once more.

In Athens, Jan Klimczak and his fellow travellers joined a group of about fifty Polish airmen and, in a Greek ship, they set out for France. On 16th October, 1939, they landed at Marseilles where they were met by a French Air Force officer. He despatched them to Brittany and a camp near Rennes, where, as a Polish unit, they served at various French Air Force stations.

In May of the following year, the mighty German war machine rolled towards the west, and once again Klimczak was on the move. After the fall of Dunkirk, along with thousands of others, he travelled south-west through France towards Spain. At the French port of St Jean de Luz an ocean liner, the *Arandora Star*, was being hastily loaded up — she was bound for England. Two attacks by German aircraft underlined the extreme urgency of the situation, and the need for rapid departure. Polish Air Force personnel were being granted priority places in the queue to board the liner, so Jan found himself on deck when the liner set

Resplendent in their French uniforms Klimczak (*centre*) and his two companions make friends with the natives.

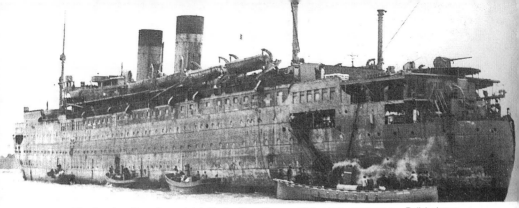

The *Arandora Star* arrives safely in England from France with its priority passengers—Polish airmen.

out to cross the Bay of Biscay on 25th June, 1940.

During that four-day trip to Liverpool, they were all surprised and amused to learn that the *Arandora Star* had been sunk with 8,000 Polish airmen on board. They landed safely at Liverpool, and for Jan Klimczak it was the end of a 5,000-mile trip.

For a time he served with 305 (Polish) Squadron, which operated Wellingtons,

as a ground electrical engineer. Then he moved to 16 Service Flying Training School at Newton, where he and five other fellow countrymen survived the crash on the moors above Edale in Derbyshire.

———

Arandora Star was later sunk by a U-boat, with the loss of many Italian internees being shipped to Canada — not one of Britain's prouder moments.

Firmly established as an important part of the RAF, men of 305 (Polish) Squadron.

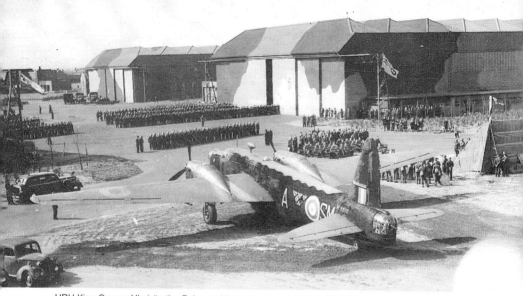

HRH King George VI visits the Poles and inspects men of 305 (Polish) Squadron.

Here the King takes the salute as a contingent of Poles march past. Note the unfamilier 'shoulder arms' position of the Short Lee Enfield rifles.

Oxford HN594, 21 Advanced Flying Unit, Seighford, on a map reading exercise, crashed on Brown Knoll, 28th December, 1945.

Map reference 082852 ● Map key number 37

The volume of air traffic over the British Isles during the early war years caused the birth of the Empire Air Training Scheme. Far away from the congestion, the relatively empty skies of Canada, New Zealand, Australia and South Africa were ideal training spaces for the aircrews of the RAF.

There was however, one big disadvantage, the crews sent abroad and trained in the clear blue skies of the Dominions, returned to this country to face the heavy cloud-choked skies of England, Scotland and Wales. It was found necessary to form special units to help acclimatise the crews to the notorious European weather conditions —they were known as AFUs (Advanced Flying Units).

Inevitably, flying accidents occurred, usually over high ground as 'Empire' trained pilots failed to cope with the low overcast, which seemed to have taken up permanent residence over Britain. This is the story of one such flying accident.

Flying an aircraft into the ground, under power, usually spelt death for the occupants, but when Oxford HN594 of No.21 AFU smashed into Brown Knoll in Derbyshire, and disintegrated, the crew of three survived. The least injured of them, Flying Officer Croker, dragged himself the best way he could over desolate moorland for over a mile to raise the alarm.

The last flight of Oxford HN594 was a routine affair, a simple map-reading exercise. Flying Officers Croker and Dowthwaite had returned from South Africa earlier in the year, and were on a course operating at Seighford, near Stafford. Converting from single-engined aircraft to multi-engined types, RAF pilots took their first step with the light twin-engined Oxfords or Ansons.

That summer had seen the end of the war, both in Europe and the Far East— the date was 28th December, 1945. It was

113

a dark showery day, with the inevitable low cloud providing ten tenths cover stretching beyond the parked Airspeed Oxford to the airfield perimeter, and on into the distance.

It was Friday after lunch that the three men, wearing their parachutes, walked unhurriedly towards the trainer. They appeared ill-equipped for flying in the middle of an English winter, for they wore no heavy flying clothing; instead they were dressed in their blue battledress uniforms. As they were on a cross-country map reading exercise they would be flying low thus avoiding the freezing conditions experienced at higher altitudes. Also the Oxford cabins were heated; it would be a reasonably short, comfortable trip—so they reasoned. It was a decision that they would shortly regret, as they lay among the shattered wood and metal on the snow covered peakland.

Warrant Officer 'Robbie' Robinson, was a pilot, navigation instructor, who was there to put the two flying-officers through a map reading test. The route that he intended to take was well known to him, for he lived in the Sheffield area. The trip was very much routine for him.

The three scrambled into the 'Ox-box' as that particular aircraft was nick-named. HN594 was an aircraft that was then getting on in years, but was still well suited to the role it played just so long as no strenuous demands were made upon it.

John Dowthwaite took up the first pilot's position (the left hand seat). He had been married in July of that year, upon his return from South Africa, and was wearing a new pair of black leather shoes, which he had last worn on his wedding day. The smart blue uniform that he was wearing was a present from his wife.

He pulled on his flying helmet and turned, asking his instructor for course directions. Robbie pulled out a map from

Warrant Officer Robinson

a pocket situated beside a folding map table, settled in the second pilot's seat and proceeded to mark out a triangular, three leg course. Because that was done by them once aboard the aircraft, no one at Seighford knew the flight path that HN594 had taken.

Ted Croker took up the third position on the seat behind the other two, situated on the main spar. He would be passenger for the first leg of the flight. Years later he was to become a Football League player and play for Charlton, and then the Secretary of the Football Association. But on that particular Friday afternoon in December, he and John Dowthwaite had the job of convincing Robbie that they could follow his scrawled pencil

Flying Officer John Dowthwaite

Flying Officer Edward Croker

lines, and match it with a flight path. At a rough guess it looked like a 140 mile trip. A couple of hours should see them back at Seighford again.

Control gave them clearance for take-off and John Dowthwaite opened the throttles; the two Cheetah engines responded by picking up to full power, and after what seemed like a good deal of runway had been used up, they were in the air and heading north-east on the first leg of the triangular flight path.

The twin-engined trainer plodded along at a mere 1,000 feet, keeping below the dull overcast with John Dowthwaite picking out landmarks and keeping to a compass bearing. As they approached the Pennine hills the ground began to rise

and the cloud seemed to drop lower. Another glance at the map told Dowthwaite that the land directly in front of the flight path rose to over 2,088 feet—he would have to climb.

A tug on his arm; Robbie was motioning him to change places with Ted Croker. With visibility deteriorating fast, John was relieved to be handing over. Robinson, in the second pilot's position took over control as the two changed places. It was time to turn onto the next leg of the planned route. As John Dowthwaite got up from his seat, he stabbed a finger at a spot height in their vicinity, indicating the danger on the map to Robbie.

Ted Croker settled into the pilot's

position and surveyed the black cloud swirling about the cockpit. Occasional glimpses of dark hills, sporting patches of snow, did nothing to ease his mind. Turning in his seat to look at John Dowthwaite, he pretended to bite his nails in mock terror. The flying conditions were a far cry from the sun-drenched skies of South Africa.

Down to business at hand and Croker spread out the map on his knees and looked at their course—Kinderscout, 2,088 feet! A glance at the altimeter told him that they would be in serious trouble if they didn't cram some space under the wings. They needed two to three hundred feet immediately.

Tilting the map towards Robinson, Croker tapped the point where Kinderscout reached maximum height. Robbie nodded and called out above the roar of the engines, "It's all right, I know this country like the back of my hand." So saying he pulled back the control column, opened the throttles and nudged the old Ox-box up through the cloud blanket.

It seemed to Croker that the old aircraft was struggling. The rev counters were showing too slow a build-up. The airspeed indicator appeared to be stuck—they were making very little headway in that

steady climb. Definitely the Ox-box was 'clapped-out' he decided. Glancing out at the port wing he could see ice forming on the leading edge—that wouldn't help matters. He was in no hurry to take over the controls from Robbie at that point; the instructor seemed to be 'unflappable'.

At a little over one hundred miles an hour the Oxford struck the top of Brown Knoll. Skidding and bouncing over the rough ground HN594 smashed itself to pieces, coming to rest one hundred and fifty feet from the point of impact. It was about 2.30 in the afternoon.

As Croker regained consciousness he decided that he was having a particularly bad dream and promptly did his best to fall back to sleep again—maybe the cold would go away. The sound of moaning brought him fully round and easing himself up, he saw that he had been thrown some distance from the aircraft. He remembered that after he had changed places with John Dowthwaite, he hadn't strapped himself in. Had he been firmly secured to his seat he would have ended up amongst the shattered and twisted wreckage. He was mildly surprised that he didn't appear to be more seriously injured. There was a dull pain in both ankles, which increased in

The remains of Oxford HN594 shortly after the accident.

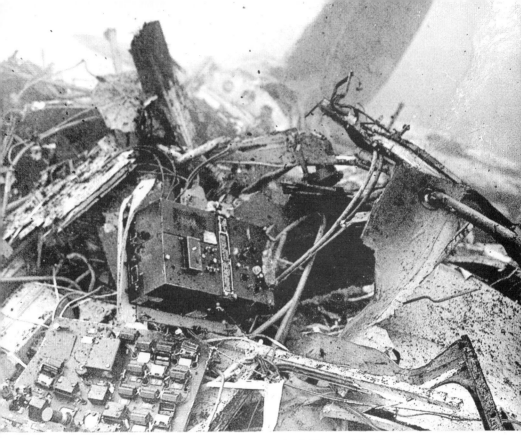

The cockpit area completely wrecked trapping Robinson and Dowthwaite.

intensity when he moved towards the wreckage to help the other two. He located them lying amidst the splintered wood and torn metal that had once been a warm and comfortable cockpit.

Of the two, Croker could see that Robbie Robinson, the instructor, was the more seriously injured. His jaw appeared to be broken and there were extensive injuries to his legs, along with some internal damage. A few feet away John Dowthwaite lay on his back with a badly smashed left leg. Still half believing that it was all a vivid nightmare, Croker began to make his companions as comfortable as he could. None of them were adequately dressed to withstand the freezing December conditions for any

length of time. Taking the parachutes that had burst open, he wrapped the two men up in them.

"Is it a dream or is it real?" muttered Croker to no one in particular.

"It's real right enough," came the reply from Dowthwaite, as he recovered consciousness.

"We are off-track . . . an air search will have problems finding us," said Croker, "and it will be dark soon." He glanced around the desolate moorland— a night out there in the depth of winter was a grim prospect. An air search would be put into operation once they became overdue, but it would likely be the next day, because by then it would be dark. Perhaps it would be days before they

117

One of the Cheeta engines and (*below*) the port wing and engine nacelle with one of the fuel tanks torn from place on the leading edge of the wing. These photographs were taken for the crash investigators.

were eventually found.

Croker made up his mind—he would have to go for help, but which way should he head? If he chose the wrong direction he could end up wandering for miles.

"Which way do I go?" He enquired hopefully of Dowthwaite.

Waving his arm vaguely in the direction of their flight path, John muttered, "That way."

Croker knew that his friend was just guessing and turning to the instructor he asked him, "Which way, Robbie?" After all, he came from Sheffield, which wasn't too far away—and he had said that he knew the area like the back of his hand.

The instructor mumbled something through a jaw that was later found to be broken in seven places, and indicated a route that would take him off the moor.

Shaking his head, Croker decided to ignore both of them and follow a strong, instinctive feeling instead. After constructing some sort of shelter for his two injured companions, he set off across the moor through the patches of snow.

It wasn't very long before he found that he couldn't bear the pain from his two ankles, and had to drop to his knees and crawl. He very soon became soaked through from the snow and clinging wet mist; the water gradually froze against his skin. The cold was becoming unbearable, especially when he stopped his exertions in order to take brief rests.

Ahead of him he could see some sheep, well protected against the elements by their thick woollen coats. If only he could get near enough to one of them, he could catch it and get some warmth from its body. The sight of a bedraggled human being crawling on all fours towards them, out of the mist, did nothing for the peace of mind of those sheep and they bounded off taking their warmth with them.

Croker pressed on, and after a while the ground seemed to be falling away until he could make progress by sliding along on his bottom. The light was fading when he found himself descending into a valley with a stream running through it. Then he spotted two houses and he was relieved to note that smoke was coming from one of the chimneys. Painfully, he dragged himself through the icy waters of the stream and up the banking towards the houses.

As he got closer he could see a Youth Hostel sign on the end of the nearest building. From that building a man emerged and walked off, away from Croker and into the dusk. No amount of shouting seemed to get his attention, but by then he was weak and his cries were faint.

After what seemed like an age, Croker reached the YHA door and with his dwindling strength, hammered upon it. There was no reply. Painfully he dragged himself on to the next house and, with frozen hands, knocked as hard as he could.

Mrs Shirt opened her front door and gasped. In the half-light she could make out a bedraggled figure of a man crouched on her doorstep. There were no shoes on his feet, no outdoor coat or hat; his clothes were soaked and torn and he was covered in dirt and mud from head to foot. The RAF wings over his left breast pocket told all—the hills had claimed yet another victim. It was getting to be a regular occurrence and her house was in the front line, situated as it was, high up the valley towards Edale Head.

Once inside, Croker shivered by the fireside and gasped out his story. Mrs Shirt would have to go about a mile down the valley to the village of Edale to get help. Before she left she asked him if there was anything that he needed.

"Just a bowl of hot water for my feet," he said through chattering teeth. With his feet in that bowl of hot water, Ted Croker passed out.

Night closed in for the two figures wrapped in parachutes lying among the

Flight Lieutenant David Crichton (Doc)
(later Air Commodore)

Opposite: Doc Crichton plans the rescue route up the moors to Oxford HN594. With him are his two wireless operators and his Motor Transport Flight Sergeant—the core of his rescue team.

broken remains of HN594. Robbie was calling for help for what seemed like hours to John Dowthwaite who lay a short distance from him. It was terribly cold, if only he could crawl nearer to Robbie they could keep each other warm through the night. John tried to move, but his legs stubbornly refused to obey his commands. Reaching down he felt his shin bone protruding through his skin.

Didn't ought to be sticking out like that, he reasoned and attempted to push it back where it rightly belonged—and fell unconscious.

It was dark as members of the Mountain Rescue Team lifted Ted Croker into the ambulance, which was parked outside the YHA building. He was out to the world, but they had to bring him round so that he could give them the whereabouts of the wreck and his two companions.

Once awake, Croker fought to stop losing consciousness, but it was difficult now that he was warm and comfortable. But it was hopeless, try as he might he could not give them the direction and possible position of HN594.

For nine hours search parties, dragging sledges behind them, scoured many acres of moorlands, intermittently flooding the area with light from flares.

After losing one of their sledges over a ravine, the rescue parties called a halt at 10 pm. The chances of coming across the two of them in the pitch darkness was remote. The search would commence again at first light.

At daybreak RAF 'planes, assisted in the search and at around 10.30 am wreckage was eventually spotted. As it turned out, the previous night's search had brought one of the parties to within four hundred yards of the crash site and the two men.

After twenty hours of lying on the open moorland, Robbie Robinson and John Dowthwaite were carried about a mile and a half across the moor, and taken to the RAF hospital at Wilmslow, Cheshire. Because of frost-bite and loss of blood the surgeons found it necessary to amputate Robbie's damaged leg.

Ted Croker had made that same mile and a half journey on his hands and knees, in about two hours. 'Not bad going', he later reasoned, especially with two badly sprained ankles.

A signal rocket is fired by the mountain rescue team to alert and encourage the injured airmen that help is on its way. (*Below*) the team sets out.

Opposite: The two injured men have their injuries attended to by Doc Crichton.

The injured are stretchered down the moor to the waiting Jeeps.

Doc Crichton carefully picks his way over the uneven ground.

Over the page: Forty years later the three survivors came together for the first time since the accident and revisited the remains of Oxford HN594. (*Left to right*) John Dowthwaite, Ted Croker and George Robinson.

*Oxford NM683, Pathfinder Navigational Training Unit, Warboys, on
a map reading exercise to Stretton, crashed on Rushup Edge, 4th
March, 1945.*

Map reference116837 ● Map key number 38

The Pathfinder Force came into being on the 15th August, 1942, and for three years was to spearhead Bomber Command's annihilation of German cities. Its members were volunteers who were carefully selected from applicant crews. Standards were of the highest and the commander of the elite force, Group-Captain Donald Bennett, was a hard task-master, who ordered the return of any crew that failed to make the grade.

Pathfinder aircraft arrived at the target first, dropping coloured markers for the 'Main Force' bomb-aimers to fix their sights on. Accurate navigation and timing were essential, with the Pathfinder pilots maintaining a correct course and airspeed, in varying flying conditions. Not only had Pathfinder crews to be determined in pressing on to targets, they also had to be unflappable types who could be trusted to drop their target indicators only when they had firmly identified the area to be bombed. Wrongly placed TIs could mean a wasted trip for the Main Force bombers who followed them in.

Every crew member's job had to be known to the Skipper so that he could make correct decisions; he also had to be above average at his own job. In particular, it was necessary for him to be a good navigator who could map read from some height. It was at his command only that target indicators were dropped. From the autumn of 1942, the success or failure of a night bombing raid depended upon the skills of the Pathfinder pilots.

During the carrying out of the raid on German Dams by 617 Squadron, use was made of a 'Master Bomber'. Wing-Commander Guy Gibson circuited the target and directed the attacks of each individual aircraft. That method was, from then on, employed by the elite Pathfinder Force. Commenting on the qualities and skills of a 'Master Bomber', *Flight Magazine* ran the following comment in its issue of 9th March, 1946:

Only men of proven ability possessing the qualities of leadership, flexibility of outlook, clear judgement and capable of immediate reaction to changed circumstances were selected for the job.

Such were the pilots of the Pathfinder Force, from among whom, were selected those individuals who acted as Master Bombers.

On 4th March, 1945, an experienced

Aircraftman Brian Gipson in his early aircrew training days.

Pathfinder pilot and Master Bomber, at the controls of an Oxford trainer, flew into the hillside above the Vale of Edale. After completing a double tour of operations with the Pathfinder Force, and earning in the process the Distinguished Flying Cross and Bar, Flight Lieutenant Brian Gipson, having survived the flak and fighters over Germany, had fallen victim to the notorious Dark Peak hills.

With the rapidly changing conditions and hill-hugging cloud masses, the Pennine hills of Derbyshire are no respecters of skilled fliers.

Upon returning from Canada, where he had trained as a pilot, Brian Gipson moved on to 1667 Heavy Conversion Unit stationed at Faldingworth. It was there that he first came in contact with the skilled organisation known as the Pathfinders. It was a recruiting drive, conducted by a pilot of that recently formed group, that caught Brian Gipson's imagination; with his crew's permission, he volunteered them.

After completing their training on four-engined bombers, they went on to the Pathfinder Navigational Training Unit at Upwood. After a week of intensive training, including many cross-country flights, he and his crew were rejected. Bitterly disappointed, they received their posting to a squadron in the Main Force, 576 Squadron, based at Elsham Wolds. It was there that Brian Gipson made his first trip over Germany, and he found it all rather exciting.

New pilots gained some experience by doing their first bombing raid as a passenger with another crew. The target for 1st January, 1944, was Berlin and along he went as second pilot — conscious that he was very much a novice. Take-off was four minutes after midnight — happy new year!

As the Lancaster approached the German capital, Brian, who didn't have any specific duties to perform on that trip, was able to take in and observe objectively all that was happening.

He looked on with calm interest as tracer shells lashed past the cockpit, and a Focke-Wulf 190, intent upon their demise, crossed his vision momentarily. It was but one of three direct attacks by fighters upon them whilst they were still in the target area. Each time, the Skipper, Flight Sergeant Thomas, managed to take drastic evasive action by diving and weaving out of trouble. Very good, thought Brian, but there was more to come.

All the ducking and weaving had taken them off track and on the return journey they inadvertently flew over the flak defences of Frankfurt. Shrapnel laced through the starboard wing and fuel lines to both engines on that side were punctured. For some reason, Flight Sergeant Thomas concluded that they were being attacked by nightfighters again, and promptly put the Lancaster into a steep dive.

Again Brian Gipson was impressed by Thomas's instant response to trouble, but wondered, mildly, about the length of time that the pilot was holding the steep dive. Voices, with the sharp edge of panic in them, were calling for the Skipper to pull up, as crew members, simultaneously, came to the conclusion that the dive had become too prolonged.

"I can't pull out!" yelled the Skipper, who was heaving back on the control column for all he was worth.

Reaching across, Brian Gipson added his strength to the task and the combined effort succeeded in levelling off the Lancaster, albeit at little more than tree-top height. During the dive the airspeed indicator needle had gone right round the clock — they must have been travelling at over 300 mph.

The crew were badly shaken and they arrived back at Elsham Wold exhausted by their ordeal. But because it was Brian Gipson's first operational flight, he assumed that every flight over Germany was like that, and consequently took it in his stride. He had found it in no way nerve-wracking, in fact, he had to admit to himself that he had enjoyed the experience; it had been exhilarating.

However, the following month on a raid to Schweinfurt, now the captain of his own aircraft, he went through another experience that was to test his flying expertise to the limit, and it was not brought about by enemy action.

On the night of 24th February, 1944, a total force of seven hundred and thirty-four bombers set out to destroy factories where airframes were being manufactured at Schweinfurt.

Gipson and his crew were running twelve minutes late, so rather than climb to the altitude of the rest of the bomber stream, he opted for catching them up at the expense of gaining height. Even at that relatively low height the rear gun turret froze up and would not traverse.

As they approached the target they could see fires blazing below. Above them, illuminated by the fires, they could see other aircraft making their bomb runs. As they were looking upwards they could clearly see a bomber passing above them from port to starboard — its bomb doors were open. As it passed directly overhead it dropped its deadly load. Gipson slipped the Lancaster sideways, but it was too late. One bomb struck the spinner on the port inner engine, another smashed through the starboard wing, in-board of number one fuel tank. A third passed clean through the fuselage on its way to the conflagration beneath, passing just a few feet away from the mid-upper turret, and its occupant. The wireless operator was sent back to examine the damage caused by the third bomb; he was advised to take a torch. It was good advice for the poor Sparks almost stepped into space through the gaping hole torn by the bomb.

Undeterred, Gipson carried on with the

run-up to target, having feathered the port-inner propellor. Once their bomb load had been dropped, Gipson attempted to re-trim the Lancaster, only to find that the trimmer had frozen solid. Consequently, he had to fly home with one foot jammed against the control column, exerting a constant force in order to keep the aircraft in level flight. Problems continued for them when the intercom packed up. The crew could no longer communicate with each other and exchange important information. The navigator scribbled his course changes on scraps of paper and passed them to Gipson. After eight hours and thirty-five minutes flying they were back on the ground — thanks to some expert flying by the Skipper.

The very next night they were sent to Augsberg to continue wrecking aircraft factories. Over the target they were picked up by searchlights and Gipson had to do some fancy flying to escape. It turned out to be the longest operational trip that they were to fly, with a duration of eight hours fifty minutes. The ancient city of Augsberg was devasted, along with the modern industrial area of the city.

Yet again, the following day, the squadron was scheduled to fly on another operation; there was a dramatic incident in the briefing hut when the medical officer marched in, stopped the proceedings and ordered them all to their beds. 576 Squadron stood down that night.

Gipson kept up his clamour to join the Pathfinder Force and at last, he and his crew received a posting to Navigational Training Unit, at Upwood. Now that they were a fully-blooded, battle experienced aircrew, they proved successful and completed the course; they received a posting to an operational squadron — 156 Pathfinder Squadron.

Some measure of the expertise that they had accrued as a team can be deduced from the very first Pathfinder

raid that they took part in.

Target for 24th-25th March, 1944, was Berlin — and it was to prove a costly one. The planners had hoped that the German defences would deduce that the target was to be Stettin and send their fighters there — but they were not fooled by the ploy. The return route took bombers to the Rhur Valley and the heavy flak concentrated in that area. Numerous aircraft drifted off course, passing over the defences, and were destroyed.

As new crews were not permitted to carry target markers on their first sortie, Gipson's crew were, in effect, 'along for the ride', accompanying the rest of the Pathfinders to 'get the feel of it'. As they approached the Danish coast they began to experience problems with the Gee navigational aid. They could have turned back, claiming faulty equipment, but Gipson opted for pressing on using dead reckoning to locate Berlin. They were all determined to do well on their very first trip with the Pathfinders, and were not about to permit a technical problem to cause them to abort. They pressed on using dead-reckoning, for there was too much cloud for them to get an astral fix.

After careful calculation, the navigator predicted that they had just crossed the coast of Denmark and gave a new course change. Carefully calculating the known wind speed and air speed, he declared that they were approaching the German town of Stettin and confidently gave a further course change. Some time passed and Gipson received a call from his navigator, "We're over Berlin!"

Members of the crew peered down in an effort to locate their position; they had arrived blind. Nothing stirred in the blackness below — where were they?

Suddenly the rear-gunner called out, "Skipper! All hell's broken out at the back!"

They had crossed the North Sea, flown over Denmark, made the correct course changes and arrived at Berlin a minute and a half earlier than the rest of the Pathfinders, using dead-reckoning. An excellent display of precision flying by anyone's standards.

Behind them, Pathfinder Lancasters were busy dropping coloured indicator flares on areas of the city to be obliterated. Support Lancasters of the Pathfinder Force were unloading further flares and incendiaries, so as to start fires for bomb-aimers in the Main Force to fix their sights on.

Realising the danger of making a tight turn, heading back towards the target centre and meeting 1,000 bombers head on, Gipson decided to make a large circuit and join the bomber stream from behind. The turn had to be a large one and by the time they finally arrived over the target, they found that they were on their own, the rest of the raiders had dropped their bombs and were on their way back home. They made their bomb run and released their cargo into the fires burning below, then turned for home, on the heels of the Main Force.

Meanwhile, a sixty miles wide swathe of bombers was thundering back across Germany making for England and safety. The German nightfighters rose to the occasion and began picking out and attacking individual aircraft, with ever increasing success. The defences were successful in destroying ninety RAF bombers.

However, for Gipson and crew, it was one of the quietest trips that they were to make throughout the war; they experienced no anti-aircraft ground fire, nor did they see any attacking fighters. The flak gunners must have been stood-down after firing constantly for over an hour at the raiders; the German fighter crews were obviously down, refuelling, resting and counting their victories when Gipson's lone Lancaster passed through their air space. So ended

Brian Gipson in his flying gear

the first sortie with the elite Pathfinder Force.

It was a mere three months later that Flight Lieutenant Gipson was selected as a Master Bomber. It was a clear indicator as to the progress and flying expertise of Gipson and his crew.

Invasion of Europe had taken place on 6th June, 1944, and Hitler was launching his V weapons at the bridgeheads in France and at the city of London. Stores of terror weapons were kept underground in concrete shelters at Wizernes, in northern France. RAF Bomber Command were called upon to locate the store of rockets and flying bombs, then attempt to destroy it. Because of the urgency and importance of the raid, it was decided to 'put it on' during the daylight. Two hundred bombers were to be involved, leading the way and directing the operation from the air was Flight Lieutenant Brian Gipson.

He had just arrived over the target when a flak burst knocked the sump off the starboard inner engine causing smoke to pour out. He eventually got the fire out and proceeded to mark the target, then circled around to direct the Main Force as they made their bombing approach. He orchestrated the whole raid and was last to leave, limping away on three engines behind the last bomber. They were so late back, and because others had seen that they had sustained damage, they were reported as having been shot down.

That attack on Wizernes was the most successful ever carried out on a doodlebug store. The Germans had cunningly concealed their terror weapons deep beneath the innocent open fields. But Gipson had located that underground store, clearly marked it, and directed every bomber individually to drop its load on exactly the right spot. All the while, they were being fired at by the ground defences and were flying with one engine knocked out.

Later that day a reconnaissance aircraft flew over the target and took pictures of the damage. The entire centre of the field had been completely caved in.

The next most demanding trip was a raid on Essen in October, 1944. Again things went wrong from the start. The bombers hit a bad weather front over the continent and windscreens began to ice up. The de-icer on Gipson's 'plane refused to function and that was followed by the failure of the H2S set (blind bombing aid). It meant that if the cloud persisted right to the target, then they would be unable to drop their sky markers (code named Wanganui). Static electricity in the clouds played havoc with their instruments, yet in spite of the problems that they were encountering, they pressed on to Essen, arriving after one hour and ten minutes blind flying. They dropped their markers and bombs on the target and turned for home; as they did so the aircraft was peppered with shrapnel from bursting flak. Upon reaching their home field, they joined the circuit awaiting their turn to land, only to discover that the undercarriage would not lower, the hydraulics had been punctured. The wheels were eventually blown down with emergency air — that landing was a tense time for the whole crew.

Another trip to Essen at the end of the year completed the required tour of operations and brought the award of Bar to the Distinguished Flying Cross for Gipson; the citation ran:

Since being recommended for the Distinguished Flying Cross, he has completed an extended tour of operations in the most exemplary manner. He has always shown a high order of skill, courage and determination and his crew has achieved a high standard of target marking over a long period. This was largely due to the fine leadership, courage and enthusiasm of Flight Lieutenant Gipson.

How then did such an experienced and skilled pilot come to smash an aircraft

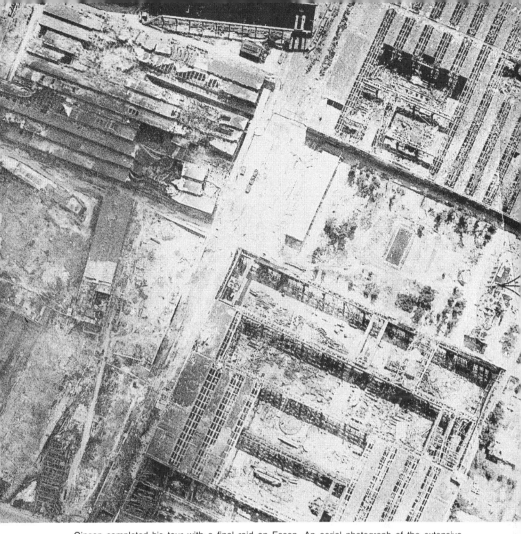

Gipson completed his tour with a final raid on Essen. An aerial photograph of the extensive damage caused to some factories at Essen.

into the Derbyshire hills in broad daylight?

The dangerous terrain of the Pennine range of hills has been stated many times However, it was during the war years that the full danger of the area for aircraft was beginning to register with the authorities. As the conflict in Europe drew to a close, the high ground in the centre of England had brought to grief over fifty aircraft, killing over seventy men and injuring many more. The area continued to claim aircraft for some ten years after the war had ended. Flight Lieutenant Brian Gipson was among the wartime victims.

After completing his tour of operations and receiving the Bar to his DFC, along with the award of the permanent Pathfinder Wings (a metal pair of wings worn over the left breast pocket, and beneath the pilot insignia), he was posted

Pilot Officer Brian Gipson, with his pilot wings and covetted Pathfinder badge.

as an instructor to the Pathfinder Navigational Training Unit, at Warboys. It was March 1945 and Nazi Germany was being squeezed on two fronts — the end was near. To Brian Gipson it seemed that the worst was over and he had survived unscathed, in a branch of the armed forces that had lost in action, one in three of its fighting men. To add to his delight, he had been posted to a unit that was based at an airfield a short distance from his home at Chatteris; things looked bright.

Because of the change in certain duties on Pathfinder bombers, the unit at Warboys was engaged in the training of engineers as map readers. Consequently, an Oxford was supplied for the job — Oxford NM683. Gipson was one of the few pilots on staff who was qualified to fly the twin-engined trainer, so he frequently got the job as pilot on the training flights. It didn't take long for the instructors to realise that the map reading trips had no pre-fixed flight plan, and therefore they could arrange to take people going on leave to their nearest aerodrome.

It was a beautiful day, 4th March, 1945, and a certain Flight Lieutenant Jones was going on leave. The nearest aerodrome for him was Stretton, Cheshire. The excuse for the trip was the training in aerial map reading of Flying Officer Skone-Reese. Flight Lieutenant Barclay was the navigation instructor and Brian Gipson was at the controls. All four were holders of the DFC — and all were most experienced and capable personnel from the elite Pathfinder Force.

It was around lunchtime when the four of them took off. Unlike the Lancaster, the Oxford carried no navigational aids, but there was little cloud about. Jones sat facing the tail and was reading a book; his helmet intercom was not connected, he didn't wish the banter of the other three to disturb his enjoyment.

As the Oxford approached the Pennine mountain chain, the cloud base began to get lower and Gipson kept below it so that the map reading exercise could continue. They were flying into the old trap. The ground began to rise gradually as the hills came closer and Gipson noticed that the altimeter was showing a mere 1,000 feet — the Oxford had entered a sandwich of cloud and ground that was rapidly closing up. Gipson realised that they were flying up a valley with cloud covered hills on either side. Suddenly, the valley came to an abrupt end, as a steep, wooded slope swept up into the grey blanket that shrouded the whole area.

He pulled back on the control column, opened the throttles and powered up into the cloud, and clear through it to blue skies. Before and beneath them, as far the eye could see, was an expanse of grey-white rolling cloud. They had no navigational aids and no idea exactly, where they were. Gipson checked the fuel gauges and noted with dismay that they were close to zero. He reached out and switched to the two emergency tanks

At the controls of an Oxford, the aircraft type in which he crashed on Rushup Edge on 4th March, 1945, whilst on a routine flight.

Brian Gipson, promoted to Flight Lieutenant, at the height of his career in the RAF. On numerous occasions he acted as 'Master Bomber' with 156 Pathfinder Squadron and yet the Pennines caught him out.

— but there was no response.

"Somethings going to have to happen soon — we're coming down anyway!" he said as he tried to get the petrol cocks to function.

"We should be clear of the Pennines by now," exclaimed Barclay, who had taken on the responsibility of navigation.

"Better that we go down under control, rather than glide down with the engines out." replied Gipson.

Losing altitude at two hundred feet per minute, he eased the Oxford down into the cloud. At the last second he saw ground rushing towards them. Yelling out, he pulled back on the stick with all his strength. That was the last thing that he remembered.

The Oxford struck the ground a glancing blow and both wings broke, bending backwards and upwards. The cockpit was shattered and the contents spilled out over the hillside.

It was raining heavily as Brian Gipson regained consciousness. There was a deathly hush, now that the two Cheetah engines had ceased. There was a quiet buzzing noise, which he immediately recognised as the giro running down; then he heard a faint groan.

The next thing he remembered was someone lifting him clear of the wreckage and carrying him to a fire engine. Then he was in a farmhouse trying to tell a policeman to get in touch with RAF Warboys. His next recollections were of clean sheets and warm blankets of the RAF Hospital at Wilmslow. His injuries consisted of a badly cut face and a broken right ankle. One of the others had a fractured backbone, but he was up and about before Brian Gipson, and shortly thereafter left the hospital.

In April, 1945, Brian Gipson was posted back to 582 Squadron, never to fly again operationally.

Since leaving the RAF, Brian Gipson held a variety of jobs. He was a dispenser for local doctors for ten years, before becoming a teacher of woodwork at Cromwell Community College, Chatteris, for twenty years. He then worked as a carpenter for a boat building firm up to his retirement.

In 1967, a painful swelling appeared on his left hand; a hospital X-ray showed up a foreign body and an operation was performed to remove it. After the operation the offending object was given to Gipson as a souvenir — it was a piece off one of the instruments from Oxford NM683. A painful reminder of the crash on Rushup Edge, on the Pennine hills in Derbyshire; a range of hills which, with their accompanying clouds, have collected some of the best pilots and crews ever to fly over this country.

Small pieces of Gipson's Oxford on Rushup Edge.

Mr Gipson in 1981 with his Distinguished Flying Cross and the certificate for the award of the Permanent Pathfinder Badge. Which was of more value to pilots than the DFC because fewer of them were awarded.

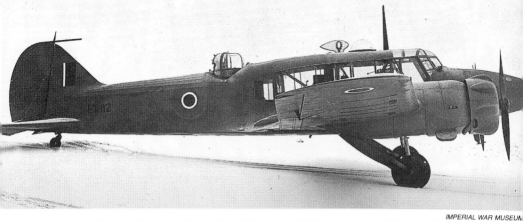

Anson N9912, 25 Operational Training Unit, crashed on Whitwell Moor, Bolsterstones, 31st March, 1941 when the wireless transmitter failed and the aircraft got off track.

Map reference 249879 ● Map key number 39

It had been a narrow escape for the crew of Anson N9912; the pilot, Pilot Officer Bernard Maurice Fournier RAFVR, had pulled off an extremely fortunate 'soft landing'. On previous occasions crews in various stages of their training had come to grief on the high ground, and the Pennine hills were to go on claiming both trainee and skilled aircrews to the end of the war and for some time after; many of them would not get off as lightly as the crew of N9912.

Although the Anson was totally wrecked the crew of four got off with scratches and bruises. The aircraft was later cleared by an RAF Maintenance Unit and Fournier's crew went on to complete their training. On that occasion they had been lucky, but their luck was to run out just a few weeks after they had begun operational flying.

The first squadron to be equipped with the Hampden bomber in 1938 was 49 Squadron operating from Scampton. However, the aircraft type was soon to prove inadequate as a bomber, its maximum load only amounted to 4,000 lb and the defensive armament was light consisting of six .303 machine-guns. It was a stop-gap aircraft that filled in until the heavy four-engine bombers got off the drawing boards and reached the operational squadrons. Pilot Officer Fournier and his crew received their posting to 49 Squadron at Scampton and the Hampdens.

During the month of August 1941 a new role was attempted for the squadrons equipped with Hampdens—intruder missions in support of the main bombing effort. Originally the Hampden had been labelled 'fighter-bomber' consequently the intruder missions were in line with that designation. However, suitability for such a role was soon shown to be lacking and the experiment was stopped in the autumn.

It was whilst engaged on an intruder mission on the night of 29th August, 1941, that Pilot Officer Bernard Maurice Fournier and his crew disappeared. The men were reported 'missing—death presumed (flying battle)' thus relatives were to wait many months in the forlorn hope that they might turn up as evaders. In the event no trace was ever found of them. At the site of their meeting up with the hills of South Yorkshire there are a few scraps of corroded metal.

Wellington R1011, 28 Operational Training Unit flying a night exercise from Wymeswold, crashed Birchen Bank Moss, January 30th, 1943.
Map reference 106987 ● Map key number 40

The official letter read, *It is with deepest sympathy that I write to tell you of your son Sgt. Raymond Gerrard Rouse, who was killed in an aircraft accident in the early hours of Saturday morning, January 30, 1943.* So began the letter of notification of the death of an experienced airman—typical of thousands of such letters that were sent to the next-of-kin during the war.

Upon joining the RAF shortly after war broke out, Raymond Rouse volunteered for aircrew duties and was trained as a wireless operator and air gunner during the summer of 1941, at 15 Operational Training Unit, operating from Harwell. In December he was posted to the Middle East and the Western Desert, where Rommel was in the process of pushing the British Army back to El Alamein and threatening Cairo and the Suez Canal. Flying as an air gunner with 70 Squadron he took part in bombing attacks on Derna and Benghazi, also against massed enemy forces and support transports using the coast road. In total he flew 41 sorties and after a brief spell with 108 Squadron he was ordered home to help train aircrews.

At the Central Gunnery School, Sutton Bridge, he passed out as a gunnery leader in December 1942. In January, 1943 he began his duties as an instructor with 28 Operational Training Unit, operating from Wymeswold. His first assignment was a daylight flight in a Wellington where his task was to oversee and co-ordinate the bomber crew's defensive fire; his next instructing flight was to be eight day's later and at night—it was to be his last.

On the night of 29th January six Wellington 1Cs took off in succession on a 'Command Bullseye' exercise. The crews were nearing the end of their training programme and would shortly be posted to front-line squadrons. The trip that night would especially test the abilites of the navigator, Pilot Officer

Grisdale, who had the task of directing the bomber on a circuitous course that would take them far north to Scotland and back to base at Wymeswold in Leicestershire. A trip that had been estimated to take from six and a half to seven hours.

The purpose behind flights of that sort was to ready RAF crews for flights of similiar duration to German cities.

The weather had been poor all day and as darkness fell worsened with the result that out of the six Wellingtons taking part in the exercise, two crashed killing some of the crew. Wellington R1538 crashed at Longton, near Stoke-on-Trent, killing two and injuring two other crew members.

Wellington R1011 was losing height as it began crossing the high ground; the crew were confident that they were on an approach to the airfield. Raymond Rouse had come forward from his position at the tail and was standing by the pilot peering into the blackness. As the most experienced man on board no doubt he felt some responsibility for the trainee crew.

At around 1.45 am Wellington R1011 dropped gently through the cloud and slammed into the moor. The three men directly at the front part of the bomber were killed instantly: Pilot, Flying Officer Lane; standing next to him, Sergeant Rouse; and in the front turret, Pilot Officer Brown.

The navigator, Pilot Officer Grisdale and Sergeant Miller survived the crash and serious injury, but were admitted to Ashton Hospital suffering from exposure.

It was the considered opinion of the commanding officer at 28 OTU that he had lost the best crew of number seven course with the crash of R1011. The letter to Sergeant Rouse's father, as next-of-kin, continued:

Your son has been putting in some sterling work as a WO/AG instructor since he came home from the Middle East and posted to this unit on the 13th September, 1942. During his tour of operations in the Middle East he carried out 41 long and hazardous flights over enemy territory, and it is very sad that on a training flight over this country an accident of this sort should happen, and he together with other members of this very promising crew are a great loss to Bomber Command.

Sergeant Raymond Gerrard Rouse

A few remains of R1011 on Birchen Bank Moss.

MIKE LAWTON

Oxford LX518, 21 (P) Advanced Flying Unit, on a night training flight from Wheaton Aston, crashed on Margery Hill, 19th October, 1943.

Map reference 180967 • Map key number 41

For Pilot-Officer Kyne it was to be his first solo night flight. He had commenced flying in Oxfords the previous month, September, 1943, and had amassed a total of fourteen hours twenty minutes on the type. He was assessed by his instructors as an 'average pilot' and was on his way to becoming a pilot in either Coastal or Bomber Command.

His training had reached that critical point in multi-engine conversion — the solo flight at night. He and his instructor had just landed after flying over the exact course that he was to attempt on his own. During his flight with the instructor, the various aerodrome lights and beacons had been pointed out. The dual flight had been successful and Kyne had acquitted himself well during it. Radio and instruments had functioned satisfactorily, as had the two Cheetah engines. Two and a half hours' worth of fuel was available in the three tanks. The weather

was good at the time and the instructor decided that all things were in order and favourable for Kyne's first solo night flight.

Before take-off, the instructor went over flight details with Kyne: he was to fly from Wheaton Aston for a distance of twenty miles west to Condover, where he would then turn due north and fly a track to Shawbury, about seven miles; from above the airfield at Shawbury he was to turn due east and fly back to Wheaton Aston — a round trip of fifty miles over a triangular course. The briefing included aids to 'Lost Procedure'; should Kyne lose his way to any of the three airfields he had recourse to a number of systems then in operation, such as 'Pundit' — code letters flashed by individual airfields; 'Darkie' — a radio emergency system; an Identification Friend or Foe transmitter (IFF); Searchlight Homing and a system known as 'Occult'.

Pilot Officer Denis Kyne RNZAF

The instructor then asked Kyne if he had any questions concerning Lost Procedure, and the trainee answered in the negative, whereupon the instructor got up from the second pilot's seat and left the aircraft. He watched as his pupil took off into the night — checking his watch he noted that it was 8.45pm.

After gaining height over the airfield, Kyne called up on the radio transmitter to Wheaton Ground Control:

"Calling Banet White, setting course for Bureau."

Those were the last known words of Pilot-Officer Kyne. 'Banet White' was the call sign for Wheaton Aston and 'Bureau' was the call sign for Condover.

There were other Oxfords flying that night and twenty minutes after Kyne had taken off, Ground Control at Wheaton became concerned on account of a deterioration in the weather. By 9.45pm it was drizzling and the call went out for all training aircraft to return.

Earlier, at 9.10pm, the beacon at Shawbury failed and remained out of action for over an hour — during that critical period, Kyne vanished.

One by one, the training aircraft landed at Wheaton until just two had failed to put in an appearance. 'Overdue' action was taken at ten minutes past midnight, and at about that time news came through that one of the missing Oxfords had landed safely at Wrexham. Still there was no word concerning LX518.

Telephone calls were put through to Royal Observer Corps Headquarters in Derby, Manchester and Leeds, to see if any of the observation posts had plotted the errant Oxford, but they were unable to shed any light on its disappearance, although the Leeds string of posts had been busy tracking sixteen Lancasters for half an hour from 2.15am.

Four days later, 23rd October, at around midday, Pilot-Officer Kyne was found in the wreckage of Oxford LX518. The site of the crash was Margery Hill, on the boundary of West Yorkshire and Derbyshire. The police at Stannington were informed and they notified RAF Norton, Sheffield, who sent an ambulance party, but they were unable to remove the body until the following day. It was obvious to the investigating officers that Kyne had died instantly, and all the signs indicated that the aircraft flew into the ground under power. There was still fuel in the tanks, but there was no way of establishing with any certainty the exact time of the crash.

It was assumed that Kyne had become lost shortly after take-off, and for some reason had failed to carry out any of the correct procedures for such an emergency. He must have gradually drifted in a north-westerly direction over an area with few airfields, and eventually over hilly country where there were no airfields at all. From the settings of instruments it could be determined that Kyne did not carry out Lost Procedure, which explains why ground stations failed to pick him up after his last radio message. He must have decided to drop through the cloud in an attempt to establish his position.

Fi103, Vergeltungswaffe 1 (V1), launched from the air by a Heinkel of Kampfgeschwader (KG) 53, aimed at Manchester, fell short and exploded near Cut Gate, 24th December, 1944.

Map reference 186965 ● Map key number 43

As dawn was breaking on the morning of 24th December, two loud explosions awoke the inhabitants of Heaton Mersey and Adswood, near Stockport. When a youngster volunteered the cause as being German flying-bombs he was quickly silenced by his elders — 'Don't talk daft lad, doodlebugs can't get this far'. Such was the disbelief among people of northern England as thirty-one V1s dropped from the skies over an area measuring 40 miles north to south and 100 east to west, from Brigg in Lincolnshire to Kelsall near Chester, taking lives and destroying property. How had the V1s, with a maximum range of around 150 miles, penetrated this far north?

Shortly after midnight about fifty Heinkel 111s belonging to the highly secret Kampfgeschwader 53 crossed the Zuider Zee at a mere 1,000 feet and, at little above wave-top height, headed out over the North Sea. Under each

An immaculately preserved V1 at Duxford on a conventional launching ramp.

Flying Bombs Over the Pennines by PETER SMITH
Model of Heinkel 111 with V1, showing method of carrying.

twin-engined bomber was slung a V1 missile, each with a warhead containing 1,874 lbs of high explosive. The target was the industrial city of Manchester.

This raid was to be the very last fling of the Luftwaffe against a northern target. Air-launching of V1s had been seen as a way of extending the range of the 'terror' weapon and hitting this country in the industrial north, thus, in some measure, retaliating for the devastation of German cities through Allied bombing. The chosen method of operation, using the reliable Heinkel 111 as carrier, was perfected by the Luftwaffe at the secret weapons base at Peenemunde on the Baltic Coast and was soon put into operation.

On the night of 8th July, 1944, coastal radar in the south of England picked up signals of incoming flying-bombs. What was alarming for the defenders was the direction from which they were coming. The missiles were flying in from the east, up the Thames estuary, and thus outflanking the extensive defence system that had been put in place to deal with the menace. Within a few weeks it was established that the bombs were in fact air launched and it was realised what the implications were for northern cities. The eyes of those reponsible for the nation's defences turned to the East Coast. Sure enough, the inevitable happened when, in the early hours of 19th September, a single V1 crossed the coast at Skegness and headed inland. It ended up blowing a crater in a potato field near Lincoln.

Not all those in authority took the warning shot seriously and at least one Home Guard AA battery was 'stood down'. Then on Sunday morning 24th December the expected big attack materialised.

An RAF operator working a set at the coastal radar station at Lowestoft picked up blips off the Lincolnshire coast. The estimated position given was 40 to 50 miles out to sea — the area selected by the German commanders as the launch point. The operator watched as the blips jumped and separated into two — then the smaller light signals began to move at speed towards the coast. After despatching their loads, each of the pilots put their aircraft into a shallow dive and one by one they disappeared off the radar screen. Group HQ at Stanmore was informed.

Crews on trawlers fishing in the North Sea had a grandstand view of many of the German aerial launchings. They were later able to report witnessing a number of failed firings, and that some of the bombs crashed down into the sea. Other missiles, with flames stabbing out behind from their tail-pipes and sounding like so many two-stroke motorbikes, flew towards the coast. Within minutes the Humber anti-aircraft defences were blazing away at the low-flying targets but failed to hit any of them, although the engines of two V1s did cut out near the coast and they hit the ground,

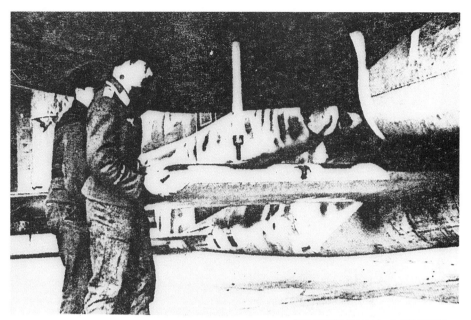

Flying Bombs Over the Pennines by PETER SMITH
V1, secured under the Heinkel's starboard wing, is being fitted with its wings.

exploding harmlessly. The attacking Heinkels had not got away unscathed as one aircraft was brought down shortly after it had released its missile. A Mosquito of 68 Squadron was responsible, and at least one other Heinkel had wounded on board as it limped home to its base in northern Germany.

Meanwhile the fearsome sound made by the pulse engines of the flying-bombs aroused people in South Yorkshire as the missiles clattered on towards their target

Flying Bombs Over the Pennines by PETER SMITH
Heinkel 111 H-16, at Ahlhorn airfield ready for a raid against this country.

147

Clearing the debris of the wrecked cottages in Chapel Street, Tottington, where six people lost their lives.

Debris in St Ann's Churchyard, Chapel Street, Tottington.

Civil Defence workers dig for victims in the rubble of destroyed dwellings at Abbey Hill Road, Oldham on Christmas Eve, 1944. Thirty-one of the dead were recovered; one body was never found. Forty-nine persons were injured in this the worst V1 explosion incident of the raid.

— Manchester. Duration of the flights of each of the bombs was no more than thirty minutes and the first one cut out and went into its dive at around 5.30am. A hen coup containing thirty birds at Chorley was blasted into oblivion. Two nearby cottages were totally destroyed, but no one was seriously injured. It was different at Oldham when another V1 dropped from the still-dark sky onto a heavily populated area at Abbey Hills Road, killing thirty-two people and injuring thirty-eight others. It was to be the most devastating explosion, in terms of loss of life, caused by the Christmas Eve raiders. Bombs were coming down all over the north with varying degrees of destructiveness of human life. There was just one fatal victim of the bomb that ploughed in at Worsley, a six-year-old boy. Seven persons lost their lives when a V1 demolished a row of cottages at Chapel Street, Tottington. Twenty-seven other houses were seriously damaged. Westwood Farm at Matley, Hyde took the full force of another V1 bringing the building down and killing two persons and injuring another three. The other fatal casualty attributed to the Christmas Eve raid was an elderly gentleman whose end was precipitated by a V1 hitting a banking at Adswood, Stockport and destroying a house and bungalow. Four others were seriously injured.

The German planners had hoped that the missiles would destroy the centre of Manchester, but only one fell within the

Plot showing the distribution of V1 impact points—the target for the flying bombs being the industrial city of Mancester

CHESHIRE — 6 BOMBS
1 Kelsall
2 Ollerton
3 Henbury
4 Macclesfield Forest
5 Stockport
6 Hyde

SHROPSHIRE — 1 BOMB
7 Newport (off map)

LANCASHIRE — 8 BOMBS
8 Oldham
9 Didsbury Manchester
10 Worsley
11 Radcliffe
12 Tottington
13 Turton
14 Oswaldtwistle
15 Brindle

DERBYSHIRE — 3 BOMBS
16 Buxton
17 Chapel-en-le-Frith
18 Beighton

NOTTINGHAMSHIRE — 1 BOMB
19 Sturton-le-Steeple

LINCOLNSHIRE — 2 BOMBS
20 Redbourne Brigg
21 Epworth

YORKSHIRE — 7 BOMBS
22 Rossington
23 Grange Moor
24 Midhope Moor
25 Sowerby Bridge
26 Willerby
27 South Cliff
28 Barmby Pocklington

COUNTY DURHAM — 1 BOMB
29 Spennymore (off map)

NORTHAMPTONSHIRE — 1 BOMB
30 Woodford (off map)

IN HUMBER ESTUARY — 1 BOMB
31 Reads Island

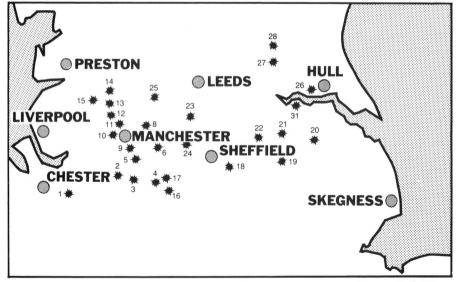

Flying Bombs Over the Pennines by *PETER SMITH*

Manchester Civil Defence Area. Eight flying-bombs exploded in the county of Lancashire, and a total of forty-two people were killed outright, with well over a hundred injured. Many private homes were destroyed or severely damaged. No factories or military targets were hit. Dr Goebbels used the raid for propaganda purposes, and had broadcast to this country on the English-speaking service that the then German offensive taking place in the Ardennes was made in conjunction with the flying-bomb attack on Manchester, the implication being that the Christmas Eve raid was the first in an all-out bombardment of northern cities. As it turned out it was a one-off raid, for failing resources, mainly aviation fuel, would prevent the Germans from attempting anything like it again.

An added feature of the flying-bombs aimed at Manchester was the inclusion of propaganda leaflets contained in cardboard cylinders in the tail of each missile. Upon the bomb entering its terminal dive a small explosive charge was intended to despatch the contents and spread them over a large area. In most cases a scattering of the leaflets did not occur and some of the containers were recovered intact, along with the

A three-storey dwelling at the end of a block of twelve houses on the north side of Abbey Hills Road, Oldham.

LIBRARIAN, METROPOLITAN BOROUGH OF BURY

Shallow water-filled crater made by the V1 on Midhope Moor

contents. Letters from prisoners-of-war were included with the direction to pass them on to relatives in the Manchester area. The idea behind the ploy was that once the relative replied to the letter, saying how they had come by it, it would indicate to the German intelligence services where the bomb had ended up, a matter of great interest to the secret Kampfgeschwader 53.

Flight paths for all the missiles in the

24th December attack lay across the Pennine Hills and one of them exploded in the Dark Peak District. A crater 40 feet across and 4 feet deep was blown in a flat stretch of moorland close to Cut Gate. The following day were still rising from the crater and all around was marked by a white deposit. The blast area is still recognisable today, although the crater rim is no longer in evidence and the crater itself is water-filled and shallow.

MIKE LAWTON

Some fragments of bomb casing near the crater.

Tiger Moth T6164, 24 Elementary Flying Training School, on a
cross-country exercise, crashed above Chew Brook, 12 April, 1945.
Map reference 034015 ● Map key number 44

The very first step for a would-be pilot in the RAF was to gain mastery and proficiency in the handling of a DH 82 commonly known as the Tiger Moth. Elementary Flying Training Schools took an individual airman to the point where he ought to be showing sufficient ability to become a pilot. If the candidate failed to fly solo after eight hours dual tution, then he was returned to the pool, where he could apply for other aircrew duties. Should he fly solo during the allotted time he went on to learn other skills such as looping, rolling, stalling, spinning and blind flying on instruments (a contraption resembling the hood of a pram was pulled over the student's cockpit for that exercise).

Leading Aircraftman M. A. O'Connell, a New Zealander, was at the end of his training with 24 EFTS; once he had passed the course he would be able put his name down for further training as either a fighter or bomber pilot. A

two-hour cross-country route would put the finishing touches to the first step in a flying career. In a few weeks the war in Europe would be over, consequently he would never get his wings in time to see active service in the Second World War.

However, he like so many others before him, whilst flying in visual contact with the ground was caught in the cloud-high ground trap and flew into the moor—he was killed instantly.

MIKE LAWTON

Colonel Stewart's immaculate Mustang, being ferried by Fredericks to Speke, crashed at Castleshaw, Oldham, at the same time as Wilhoit crashed at Glossop.

Mustang P51D, 44-64084, 336 Fighter Squadron, 4th Fighter Group, USAAF, ferrying from Debden to Speke, crashed at Glossop 29th May, 1945.
Private land ● Map key number 45

The war in Europe ended on 8th May, 1945 and at the USAAF fighter station at Debden, Essex, twelve P51D Mustangs with less than 100 hours flying time were selected to be flown to Speke, Liverpool. From there they were to be crated and shipped to the States and finally to the Pacific theatre of war.

The final mission flown by the unit, 4th Fighter Group (Debden Eagles), had been on 25th April when the Group commander, Colonel Everitt W Stewart, had led a fighter sweep as far as Czechoslovakia, encountering the much-vaunted Me262 German jet fighter and plenty of flak. The Colonel's personal aircraft, 44-72181, named *Sunny VIII*, was one of the fighters selected for packaging and return. The aircraft's name was painted in red and outlined in black; the spinner and nose was bright red; engine cowling, canopy frame and rudder were painted light blue. On the canopy frame were painted eleven small swastika emblems, indicating victories scored whilst Colonel Stewart was flying with

355th Fighter Group. He took over command of the Eagles in February 1945.

First-Lieutenant Beacham O Brooker (Beach) and First-Lieutenant Harold H Fredericks were close friends and volunteered to help fly the low-mileage P51Ds to Speke. They had an ulterior motive, as had a number of other pilots who also volunteered, for they intended to spend a few days in Blackpool after delivering their charges, before re-turning to Debden and the monotony of peace-time flying routines.

Fredericks was to be 'Horseback', that is, leader of the flight of twelve red-nosed fighters; his buddy Beach would be flying in the Number 3 position. Lieutenant Beach Brooker was especially looking forward to a few days' break at the holiday resort. He had just turned 21, and since he had completed his tour of missions by VE day he could expect an early return Stateside.

On the morning of 29th May, 1945 the crew chief for *Sunny VIII*, Sergeant G H Weckbacher, was there to hand over his charge to Fredericks. He recalled that the commander for the ferrying flight was uneasy. The weather was grim and Fredericks expressed his fears that someone might get killed, that there was high ground along the route and really, the flight ought to be postponed. It was obvious to the crew chief that the lieutenant just didn't want to go.

Disgruntled, Fredericks stepped up into the cockpit of the immaculate fighter and stowed away his valise behind the pilot's seat. Sergeant Weckbacher handed him the necessary forms for hand-over and delivery, then stepping back off the wing onto the ground he watched as *Sunny VIII* was taxiied into the wind before powering off down the runway. When he had been assigned as crew chief for 44-72181 Colonel Stewart had had told him, "I want this to be the best-looking airplane on the field." He, along with the other two ground crew men, Brown and Young, had seen to it that the Mustang shone and sparkled, its paintwork unmarked. They had been proud of their charge, and now it was on its way to the Pacific.

By 10 o'clock all twelve fighters were airborne, in formation and heading for the west coast — a distance of 160 miles. Near Leicester they encountered thick cloud and Fredericks, as 'Horseback' for the flight, instructed them to climb to 6,000 feet. They were no longer in sight of the ground. He made several attempts to raise Speke but was unsuccessful, he being the only pilot with a wireless

Colonel Everitt W. Stewart, commander of 4th Fighter Group, 'Debden Eagles'.

directly in contact with ground control at Speke. The rest were on squadron channel and only able to contact each other.

After 55 minutes had passed by, Fredericks estimated that they should be over Speke and, with ice forming on flying surfaces, he opted for descent through cloud. His last instructions were, for the pilots to look out for any 'dromes as they came out of the clouds. Beach, who was tucked in close to Fredericks in the Number 3 position, recalled the events that followed:

"As we were letting down through the overcast Fredericks' plane suddenly disintegrated in front of me and a ball of fire flung my plane to one side. Immediately I pulled up out of the soup and found that my aircraft was difficult to handle. Looking out at my port wing I saw the reason why, two feet had been ripped away.

"I called up Douglas Groshong, who was leading one of the flights, and told him what had happened. I said that I might have to bale out as I was experiencing difficulty in flying straight and level. First I would see if the fighter could be handled at landing speeds; I lowered the undercarriage and flaps and tried a few stalls. Satisfied that I could safely bring off a landing I told Groshong that I was turning back for base and called for 'homing' assistance."

Most of the others who had gone down through the murk carried on and found Speke in poor visibility. Some opted for climbing back into the cloud and seeking another opening. Others became separated from their flight leaders and turned back for Debden.

The hills were to claim another victim from among the Mustangs. Flight Officer Darnaby H Wilhoit, flying 44-64084, was to be the second victim. He decided for descent and sight of the ground whilst still over the hills. Under considerable power he flew into the ground off Monks Road, Glossop.

Two mighty explosions brought people running from their houses. First to reach the blazing wreckage was a young boy, Walter Mason, followed by a member of the Land Army, Mrs Alice Walker. Getting as close to the flames as they could they made attempts to smother the fire with earth, until they discovered the body of the pilot. Mrs Walker spotted some papers and a New Testament, which she managed to snatch seconds before the flames reached them.

Wilhoit's crash site is within the Dark Peak area but is on a farmer's land; larger portions of wreckage were recovered at the time.

Fredericks had ploughed into the moors at Castleshaw, north of Oldham. Although it is outside the area of the Dark Peak National Park, because of the high ground and difficult access some wreckage of *Sunny VIII* still remains at the site.

Fredericks was an experienced pilot with 315 combat flying hours, all with 4th Fighter Group. When he was killed he was serving as assistant operations officer with 336 Squadron, which he had joined in February 1944. He was officially credited with three enemy aircraft destroyed, with a part claim on a Me262 jet. He had been posted to the elite fighter group at about the time that the three squadrons comprising 4th Fighter Group were making the change from P47 Thunderbolts to P51 Mustangs. Despite some initial teething troubles with the fighter the Group began to score heavily against the Luftwaffe. The increased range meant that the fighter pilots could reach deep into Germany in their escort duties for the heavy bombers. It also meant that they could seek out German airfields and strafe aircraft on the ground, thus adding to their total of 'kills'.

There was a competition between two

(*Left*) First Lieutenant Harold H. Fredericks flew into the ground at Castleshaw, Oldham.

USAAF Groups for the highest number of victories over the Luftwaffe; 56th Fighter Group, known as the 'Wolf Pack' and equipped with Thunderbolts, vied with the 'Debden Eagles' for supremacy — each month the kills were totted up. In the March of 1944 the Wolf Pack was ahead of the Eagles with 400 kills to 300, but with their Mustangs they were confident of catching up and passing their rivals.

The Eagles were led by the dynamic fighter ace Colonel Don Blakeslee, who was determined that his Group end up as top scorer. Fredericks was involved in the drive for victories over the FW190s and Me109s and during April they managed to get ahead of the rival Group.

As the month of June began the pilots were briefed for the invasion of the Continent and black and white stripes were painted on the wings and fuselages; two small bombs were fitted to each aircraft. With the invasion underway on

6th June Fredericks was engaged in a fighter-bombing sweep over French countryside. Whilst flying low near the German airfield at Evreux he was caught by some accurate anti-aircraft fire and brought down. After crash-landing he was contacted by the French Resistance, who helped him to evade capture and escape to Spain.

He reached England and returned to his unit by September, 1944. Usually, following a successful return of a downed pilot, they were kept from flying on missions until the people who had helped them had been liberated. By the time that Fredericks was allowed to fly on missions again the Eagles had taken their score to 700. The race was on to be the first Group to reach 1,000 kills.

During October a number of V1s exploded in the vicinity of Debden and the story got round that Goering was trying to hit the 'Red Nosed Gangsters' so as to save his precious Luftwaffe. The

First Lieutenant Beacham Brooker's aircraft with damage to its port wing-tip; he almost flew into the ground, close behind his leader

following month 16 replacement pilots arrived at Debden from the states, among them was Beach Brooker. Out of those 16 new pilots eight would be shot down and either killed or taken prisoner before the war ended.

Beach got into the shooting war when he strafed a train and some 50-plus German soldiers taking cover in a ditch were killed. His first air victory came when he was engaged in the shooting-up of Kothen aerodrome near Berlin — *and he was vectored onto the FW190 from the ground.*

One of the 336 Squadron pilots, 'Swede' Carlson, had got carried away in his enthusiastic strafing of a four-engined aircraft standing at dispersal and had misjudged his height. Hitting the ground, he had crash-landed on the edge of the field. Carlson remained in his cockpit cursing his luck as red-nosed fighters whipped back and forth across the 'drome shooting at everything in sight, causing fires in hangars and other buildings. Then he heard someone over the R/T mention that a Mustang was down and ought to be shot up so as not to fall into German hands. That galvanised Swede Carlson into action, and leaping up he called out that he was still with the kite and that they had better leave him alone or else.

In all the confusion around the aerodrome two FW190s were trying to slip in for a landing unnoticed. Swede spotted them and standing on the wing of his downed fighter he called up the leader, McKennon, and told him about the FW190s. He was able to give a running commentary of the German fighters' positions as they sought to put down. The first Mustang to spot them fired at the leading aircraft and then overshot. Beach, following up behind, made absolutely sure and raked the fighter, causing it to spin into the ground. The dead German pilot was a man named Hoffman, commander of the aerodrome

— it was Beach Brooker's first kill. The German soldiers defending the aerodrome were infuriated at the way Swede had directed the attack on the fighters; according to them, once he was down the war was over for him, yet they had heard him on the radio. He begged to differ.

Because of the increasing appearance of the German jet fighter, the Me262, four RAF Gloster Meteors arrived at Debden to give the 4th some experience of flying against jets, and for them to develop some counter-measures. In combat the Me262 could leave the Mustang standing, and should they begin appearing in any great number, even at that late stage in the war, the RAF and the 'Mighty Eighth' would be in trouble.

On 4th April, 1945 the Group was detailed to fly protection on some B-24s that were on a bombing mission deep into Germany. It was around 10 o'clock in the morning and the red-nosed fighters had been escorting the bombers for about one hour when the cry went up 'bogies at five o'clock'. As the bombers were nearing their target eight Me262s came up at the formations from below and behind. At once the protecting fighters pounced on the attackers and two of the much-vaunted jets were sent down in flames. When another three launched an attack on the bomber stream some minutes later four Mustangs ganged up on one of them and knocked it down — Fredericks was one of the pilots who claimed a share in the kill.

Rivalry between the Eagles and the Wolf Pack hotted up during April, as it became obvious that the war might end at any time and the 'magic' 1,000 kills might not be reached. The Eagles were to be frustrated when on 11th April, they came upon a 'drome packed with parked aircraft, and yet were ordered not to strafe. Two days later they heard that the Wolf Pack had hit Eggebek airfield and succeeded in destroying 90 on the ground, thus pushing their score to 1,002. They

(Right) First Lieutenant Beacham Brooker 'Beach' hit the ground with his port wing and managed to keep in the air. Upon landing safely he climbed out of the cockpit, thoroughly shaken, and never piloted an aircraft again.

had won that particular race, but which Group would end up top scorer when the war ended?

The chance to beat the Wolf Pack once and for all presented itself on 16th April. German aircraft were being flown back from locations on all fronts to the few remaining fields in German hands. Short on fuel and pilots, the aircraft remained where they had been parked-up, sitting targets for the strafing fighters. Debden Eagles destroyed 105 of them, but not without loss to themselves. German aircraft were concentrated, but so were the anti-aircraft defences, and eight Mustangs were brought down. Such was the eagerness to become fighter aces before the end came. Beach claimed two Me410s destroyed on the ground.

With kill figures still to come in by the end of the war, on 8th May, from downed pilots, who were either prisoners-of-war or were still in the evader pipe-line, the top scoring Group appeared to be the 56th. The Wolf Pack were claiming 1,008 victories as against 1,003 for the 4th.

Members of 336 Fighter Squadron; Beacham Brooker is standing first row, fifth from left.

(*Right*)Flight Officer Darnaby H. Wilhoit, crashed at Monks Road, Glossop, in P51D, 44-64084, the first of two to be killed on the flight to Speke.

However, when the final tally was made the Eagles came out on top with a grand total of 1,016 enemy aircraft destroyed.

Barnaby M Wilhoit had arrived too late at the 4th Fighter Group to have a share in the final score; he had joined at the end of March, just five weeks before the war ended and eight weeks before his fatal accident.

On 4th November, the pilots of the famous 4th Fighter Group sailed on the *Queen Mary* for home. It had seen its beginnings in three RAF squadrons, 71, 121 and 133, when American volunteer pilots had travelled to Britain to join in the war against Hitler. When the United States came into the war and its forces arrived in this country the three squadrons were taken over in the late summer of 1942. They were redesignated 334, 335 and 336 Squadrons respectively, becoming the 4th Fighter Group — the Debden Eagles, the elite fighter group and top-scorers of the Mighty Eighth.

Crash site of Fredericks's aircraft at Castleshaw.

BRIAN ROBINSON

Barracuda MD963, Station Flight, Dunino, Scotland, crashed at Redbrook Clough, 29th July, 1945.

Map reference 024103 ● Map key number 46

Pilots who flew the Royal Navy Barracuda and who had been used to its predecessors, the Albacore and the stately Swordfish, were often caught out by this replacement monoplane, torpedo bomber. It could not be flown with the same casualness as the biplanes that it was superceding. There had been fatalities among the pilots of the squadrons first equipped with it. The Barracuda had earned for itself a bad reputation.

It was the Royal Navy requirements and specifications that were directly reponsible for Fairey Aviation producing this aircraft of odd appearance. Because observation of the sea beneath was considered first priority, the Barracuda's wings were placed high; the fuselage appeared to be slung under a single wing, which was interrupted by a long, awkward-shaped, cockpit cupola. The tailplane had to be positioned high on the fin, so as to avoid turbulence from the

wing, but that meant that supporting struts were needed, which in turn added to drag.

Furthermore, high placed wings meant that the designers had to come up with a large undercarriage, which could be retracted into the underwing surfaces. The ungainly undercarriage structure had to be robust enough to withstand repeated deck landings—yet more weight. Because the overly large undercarriage created tremendous drag, pilots, naturally, wished to retract it as soon as they were airborne. However, because the clumsy contraption folded the wheels into the leading edge of the wing, airflow was interrupted, resulting in lift being lost for a few vital seconds during take-off. The Barracuda would suddenly drop a few feet until the wheels were safely housed.

The hydraulic system required to operate the undercarriage was tremendous, and worked at a pressure of

2,500lb per square inch. Consequently, there were frequent failures of the system and hydraulic fluid would be distributed in all the wrong places, with resulting damage.

In flight the Barracuda was unstable and had to be flown under the pilot's control all the time. Pilot's notes for the awkward looking aircraft, under the heading 'High Speed Stall', carried the following warning:

If the aircraft is stalled in a steep turn either wing may drop sharply, but recovery is almost immediate when the pressure on the control column is relaxed.

On 29th July, 1945, a Royal Navy Barracuda, in the process of executing a tight turn over moorland in the vicinity of Marsden, slipped into the ground killing the only occupant, the pilot, Sub-Lieutenant Ambler.

Ambler lived in Sheffield and he may have intended flying over his home city. It was a common desire of service airmen to make a trip over their homes. As the war in Europe was coming to its end, and during the immediate post-war period, understandably, there was a more relaxed atmosphere in the services. Eleven aircraft came to grief in the Dark Peak from the Spring to the end of December, 1945 — the Pennine chain of mountains remained impervious and unforgiving.

Mr J W Wood, a blacksmith of Bleak Hey Nook, near Standage, was witness to the crash of Barracuda MD963. It was just after one o'clock in the afternoon and Mr Wood was walking across the moors with his dog, when he heard an aircraft approaching. At first he could see nothing as there was low cloud and a ground mist. Suddenly, it appeared through the mist at a mere hundred and fifty feet, went into a tight turn, a wing dropped and the aircraft plunged into the hillside. A cloud of blue smoke shot upwards and the Navy 'plane erupted into a mass of flames.

There was nothing that Mr Wood could do to save the pilot, who must have been killed instantly. He raced over to the Great Western Hotel, and from there he telephoned the West Riding Police.

At the the crash site, on the very edge of the Peak District, very little remains to be seen of the weird looking aircraft, the Fairey Barracuda, of which a famous story is told. It is said that an American general, who was being shown the Barracuda for the first time, took up a close examination of it, walking round and round it, then standing back he declared: "That's the finest flying machine that I have ever seen, but it will never replace the airplane."

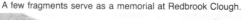

A few fragments serve as a memorial at Redbrook Clough.   MIKE LAWTON

Meteor RA487, 66 Fighter Squadron, Linton-on-Ouse, on a night flying exercise, crashed on Hagg Side, 8th December, 1950.

Map reference 165891 ● Map key number 48

Crowds throughout Britain today are thrilled by the displays and incredible aerobatics performed by the world famous Red Arrows, almost always the highlight of any aviation event.

The precision flying programme, with its daring high speed manoeuvres, has evolved since the Second World War and the arrival of the jet aircraft. Prior to the RAF Red Arrows, who today operate with Hawk trainers which superceded their Folland Gnats, were the Black Arrows and Blue Diamonds with their Hawker Hunters.

However, an aerobatic team had been thrilling spectators during the early post-war years. Flying the first operational jet fighter, 66 Squadron were pioneers of jet flight, precision aerobatics, for the pleasure of the general public.

A member of that aero-formation team became lost over Derbyshire, and with his fuel gauges registering zero, he baled out. His Meteor Mk4, still under power, crashed into a wooded hillside in the Derwent Valley.

Sergeant-Pilot Joseph Harrington joined the RAF in 1943 and was assessed as suitable for pilot training. After introductory training and 'useful duty' service, he went to Canada in the Spring of 1944 to flying school. As the war drew to a close, Joe Harrington returned to this country and was given a choice — either to serve as a glider pilot, or to go on a pilot/flight-engineer course for Lancasters. As unpowered flight held little appeal to Joe he finally opted for the heavy bombers. Following a peacetime tour on Lancasters, he converted to the larger Lincolns, and finally left the service in 1948.

In the immediate post-war years, civil aviation companies were being swamped

with applications from ex-bomber pilots for positions with their airlines. Joe made his attempt to carry on flying and joined the flood of applicants. However, ex-Transport Command pilots were receiving priority, as they were considered likely to have the steady experience required to handle civilian freight and passengers.

The answer to Joe seemed simple enough—re-enlist as a pilot in Transport Command then, after serving a period with them, leave and once again apply to one of the civil airlines that were springing up everywhere. In October, 1949, Joe re-enlisted on a four year aircrew engagement—it was a bit drastic—but he dearly wished to be an airline pilot. After a refresher training course he was assessed as suitable for Transport Command—he had made it and was on his way to realising his ambition.

On 25th June, 1950, North Korean troops crossed the 38th Parallel and advanced into South Korea. As a consequence, RAF fighter squadrons were being strengthened and Joe found himself on a conversion course to fly the Meteor twin-engined jet fighter, with little say in the matter. So much for Transport Command and eventually a captain's job with a civil airline.

In what seemed like no time at all, Joe found himself a fully-fledged fighter pilot and on the strength of 66 Squadron, stationed at Linton-on-Ouse. The accident rate was high on the new jet squadrons and 66 Squadron had its share of fatalities.

Formation aerobatics were to prove dangerous and on one occasion during a display, Joe collided with another Meteor over their home base, but fortunately he managed to bring the fighter and himself down in one piece.

Under the leadership of Pilot Officer Murphy, 66 Squadron produced a good flying formation team, which gave many

(*Left*) Sergeant Joseph Harrington.

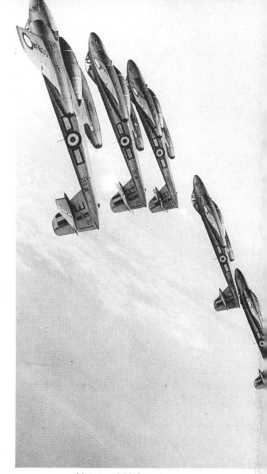

Meteors of 66 Squadron.

displays at RAF stations and at 'Battle of Britain' week. The way was being paved for the dramatic air displays that we see today.

It was in the winter of that year that the commanding officer of 66 Squadron, Squadron Leader A. Lang, DFC, decided to give his men some experience in flying at night. At some future time, there was the very real possibility that the Squadron may be called upon to take-off in the evening and land in darkness.

On 8th December, 1950, Joe took off from Linton; the course that he had been given was a triangular one. He was to fly the first leg to Manchester, then turn due

A classic scramble by pilots of 66 Squadron.

east to a point in East Yorkshire, where he was to make a further course change that would bring him back to base. Simple enough when you can see the ground, but on that particular night there was a layer of cloud covering most of the country. The navigation was mainly a matter of steering a heading for a certain length of time, at a constant speed, with radar service as back up.

After the appropriate amount of time had lapsed, Joe, guessed that he must be over Manchester, although he had no visual confirmation, and made the course change to head east.

It was during the second leg that he discovered that his four-channel VHF set had become unserviceable, which meant that he would be without radar assistance for the remainder of the flight. Around that time he calculated that he should be making his next course change and turned north. It was no use he decided, he would have to drop below cloud and try to verify his position.

He was unable to recognise a single feature in the darkened countryside beneath him, as it flashed by. A glance at his fuel gauge and he knew that he was in serious trouble, he had spent too long trying to verify his position. He had only a few minutes left before the two Derwent engines sucked in the last few gallons of kerosene. He switched the IFF set to 'distress', although he doubted that any ground station would pick up the signal.

What was he to do next? A long, straight stretch of road came into sight; he decided to attempt a landing on that, it was a better proposition than baling out. He should try to save the aircraft if at all possible, after all, it had cost the taxpayers plenty. He flew a low pass over the road to warn any traffic, and make a closer inspection of the surface and surrounds.

Suddenly, off the starboard wing tip a factory chimney loomed into view; it was too close for comfort, and he decided there and then to abandon the fighter rather than try to land it. Having made his decision he recalled an incident which had occurred three days before.

The commander of their sister squadron at Linton (92 Squadron) had run into trouble and had tried to bale out—and had tragically met his death. The cockpit on the Meteor was well forward, affording the pilot an excellent view of the ground, however, it meant that leaving the cockpit in full flight was especially dangerous as there was a good chance of being hit by the leading edge of the wing.

With that very much in mind, Joe ran through all the correct procedures—he would stick to the book; the experts who had set out the correct procedures had to be trusted. He climbed the fighter to a good height, using up the last dregs of fuel.

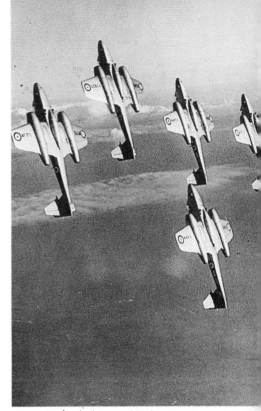
Aerobatic team of 66 Squadron.

"I climbed to around 5,000 feet above the cloud, disconnected my headset, throttled back, put down one third flap, trimmed the aircraft and then put it into a shallow turn to the left.

"I was halfway out of the cockpit when the aircraft began to descend, and I found myself jammed and unable to move any further out. The only thing remaining for me to do was to get back into the cockpit and try again. Having readjusted the trim and climbed onto the seat, I launched myself over the wing and fell under the tail in true text-book manner.

"I found myself tumbling through the sky and after several hasty attempts to pull the ripcord, I calmed down and as I fell began to search for it—located it and gave it a good tug.

"When the 'chute had fully opened and

Straight and level, Joe Harrington in 'S' for Sugar.

was blossoming above me, I was able to look down and was able to recognise that I was over hilly country—so I prepared myself for a rough landing. I heard an explosion somewhere beneath me and just hoped that the aircraft had crashed in open country.

"My feet touched the ground and I fell flat on my face into, what turned out later to be, a ploughed field."

After disconnecting his parachute, Joe examined himself and found that, although he was shaken, he was uninjured. His light flying overall was covered in mud and he was missing one of his flying boots. He peered all around into the dark December night and discerned a twinkling light in the distance. Climbing over a fence, he limped across a number of fields towards, what was turning out to be, a cluster of farm buildings.

A middle-aged lady opened the door to his knocking—she looked him up and down without saying a word. Joe realised that he must have presented a terrifying sight and hastened to reassure her.

"Good evening," he said, "I'm very sorry to disturb you but, I've just had to bale out of my aeroplane and I need help."

"Oh, please come in and have a cup of tea," responded the woman, as though mud-plastered airmen made a habit of dropping in on her.

Eventually, Joe was taken to the police station at Hope, in Derbyshire, where he began to clean himself up. They gave him some soup and after a couple of hours an RAF flight lieutenant arrived to drive him to RAF Finningley, where he spent the night. Next morning Joe was given a lift to Linton-on-Ouse where, upon arriving through the Mess door, he was given a standing ovation by the other

Members of 66 Squadron Aerobatic Team, with Joe Harrington on the far right

squadron members. The only person who seemed to be put out by Joe's survival and return was the NCO in charge of the parachute stores. Sergeant Joe Harrington should have held on to his ripcord handle and brought it back with him, but, in all the excitement, he had lost it. Well, Joe reasoned, there's just no pleasing some folks.

After completing more than the usual time on a peacetime tour with 66 Squadron, Joe was given the choice of becoming an instructor, or 'doing target towing at Acklington, Northumberland. As that town was not far from his home, he chose the latter option and was posted to Northumberland.

Between his target towing duties out over the North Sea, Joe was able to study for his Civil Licence, with the eventual aim of achieving his ambition to become a civil airline pilot.

Upon leaving the RAF he was successful in his ambition, and joined Swissair as a captain flying DC8s.

When he left his Meteor over Derbyshire that December night, RA487 plunged into a plantation on Hagg Side, creating a deep crater. Although much of it was cleared, pieces of impacted metal and armour plate, along with instrument cables and wires, remain in a crater at the site.

The remains of Joe's aircraft, in a pine wood, in the crater caused by the crash in December, 1950. *MIKE LAWTON*

Consul TF-RPM, on a delivery flight to an Icelandic airline, crashed on Crow Stone Edge, 12th April, 1951.

Map reference 174967 • Map key number 47

A lone hiker, Ronald Yates of Pitsmoor, Sheffield, was walking across Crow Stone Edge on Howden Moors, when he caught sight of an aircraft fuselage and tail sticking up in the air. Amongst the wreckage he found the bodies of three men—they appeared to have been killed instantly.

On the morning of 12th April, 1951, Consul TF-RPM took off from Croydon, its destination was Iceland, a journey of 1,750 miles. The course was to be via Liverpool and Prestwick.

The aircraft had been built in 1942 by Airspeeds at Portsmouth, and had begun its life as Oxford HN471, a trainer with the RAF. After the war it was re-purchased by Airspeed and underwent conversion for a civilian role, as a light transport and was fitted out to seat six passengers. Extra windows were installed, double doors were fitted to cut off the cockpit area and a longer nose

fitted to accommodate luggage. In its Airspeed livery of dark blue and gold, it was purchased by an Icelandic airline company for around £5,500, and was on its delivery flight.

The pilot, Pall Magnusson, aged twenty-six, from Sentiarnarnesi, Iceland, had received a weather report from the Meteorological Office suggesting winds of up to sixty mph and that conditions were unfavourable for visual flying.

However, for some reason, rather than use instruments, Magnusson opted for visual flying. That meant keeping in sight of the ground and map-reading his way along the planned route. Over the Pennines, in the area of the Dark Peak, a near gale was blowing.

Acting as wireless operator was an Englishman, Alexander Watson, aged forty-two, of Leytonstone, London. Watson was on loan to the Icelandic air company from Morton Air Services

Limited of Croydon.

Flying as passenger was another Icelander, Johann Rist, aged thirty-five.

The site of the crash on Crow Stone Edge was 1,600 feet above sea level, and some forty miles east of the planned course. A senior investigator for the Ministry of Aviation Accident Investigation Branch, who examined the remains of the aircraft at the site, reported that in his opinion there had been no structural failure or mechanical breakdown prior to the crash. He also expressed the opinion that the engines had been under some considerable power when the Consul impacted with the moor.

As the pilot had not requested a change from visual to instrument flying, nor apparently, had he broadcast distress calls, it was concluded that he had been taken unawares. He had fallen into the same trap as so many other pilots when flying in the vicinity of the Pennines.

The Consul would have started out with the pilot confidently flying under the clouds and in sight of the ground. Then, with the ground rising gently until it was swallowed up in the clouds, he would have climbed above the overcast. After having opted for the easier visual contact with the ground method, rather than navigating with the use of instruments, he would have found himself flying blind with no idea of his position. At some point he would have assumed that he was clear of the high ground and begun a descent. He would have expected to be able to pinpoint his position and make any needed adjustment to put him on course for Liverpool.

Winds of around seventy miles an hour had slowed forward progress and pushed the Consul into the heart of the Peak District, where clouds and ground all too frequently meet.

One of the Cheetah engines belonging to the Consul—stripped by souvenir hunters.

MIKE LAWTON

Vampire DH100, RAF Finningley, crash-landed on Moscar Top, 300 yards from the Strines Inn, 25th July, 1951.

Map reference 218899 ● Map key number 49

Staying with a striken aircraft and risking a crash-landing is a lottery; especially so when the ground is uneven—the risk of fire is great; so to hit the ground and for the aircraft to burst into flames and the pilot survive is fortunate in the extreme.

In the case of the Vampire which made a 'soft landing' on Moscar Moor Top the first person to reach the scene and render aid to the pilot was a member of Sheffield Ambulance Service. Mr W. H. Livesey, who lived at Sugworth actually saw the twin-boom fighter drop through the clouds and bounce across the moorland. Immediately he was able to dial 999 and alert the emergency services, after which he grabbed his First Aid equipment and raced up the moor.

He could see the pilot still in the cockpit and the canopy was being lifted back as he drew closer. Ominous cracklings and sputterings were coming from the engine area behind the cockpit and smoke was beginning to billow up as the pilot, Flying Officer Beckford, scrambled clear and fell into his rescuer's arms.

With a loud bang the Vampire errupted into flames with the pilot and Mr Livesey a safe distance away. He applied a dressing to Beckford's badly grazed knee and cleared dirt from his eyes; he then helped him down to the road and along to Sugworth Hall where he was given a cup of hot tea.

Sheffield Fire Brigade arrived at the scene but by that time the Vampire had burnt itself out. Little remains at the site today apart from lumps of heat-fused metal.

Wellington MF627, 6 Advanced Navigation School, on a cross-country exercise from RAF Lichfield, crashed Ughill, 17th October, 1952.

Map reference 265892 ● Map key number 42

Take-off time was 11.55pm and at the controls of Wellington MF627 was Sergeant Reginald Keith; Pilot-Officer David Ward was navigator and Pilot-Officer Brian Thirkell was second navigator.

After three hours the flight was nearing its end and Sergeant Keith was in contact with Lichfield. They were about to enter the circuit prior to landing. The ground was obscured by low cloud and fog, so the final approach was being made on the Gee homing system. In accordance with normal procedure, the pilot asked the second navigator to come up front to be a second pair of eyes and to assist if necessary.

Brian Thirkell moved into the cockpit, sat in the flight engineer's seat and fastened the six-inch wide strap across his chest. He recalled the events that followed:

"I remember Sergeant Keith saying to me, 'Look out for the ground'. So confident were we of our position in relation to Lichfield, that the undercarriage was down and flaps partially lowered.

"Both of us saw the ground rushing up at the same moment. The pilot rammed on the power; I lept forward, grabbed the throttle levers and held them. Sergeant Keith pulled back on the control column and we ploughed into the ground in an upward slide.

"Coming to rest, the pilot and I scrambled out through the roof of the cockpit, virtually unharmed, and surveyed the scene. We were on quite a

slope, surrounded by swirling mist and under observation by some puzzled sheep. The tail section, still upright, had come to rest some distance from the main wreckage. One of the engines had rolled off down the hill and the fuselage, aft of the main spar, was split wide open.

"From within the shattered aircraft we could hear the moans of David Ward, so we scrambled in to get him. We carried him out and placed him on top of the upturned dinghy, which had self-inflated upon impact; he was semi-conscious."

Thirkell stayed with Ward whilst Keith went for help, following some overhead cables. Some time later he returned with a farmer and contingents from the fire and ambulance brigades.

Wellington MF627 had crashed fifty miles north of where the crew thought they were. The subsequent inquiry did not hold either navigators responsible, as they were not considered qualified, that left Sergeant Keith. As pilot in command and as the only qualified crew member, he was held responsible for the loss of the aircraft. As it happened, there were no serious injuries to the three crew members.

Some bits and pieces that were collected from the crash site in recent years.

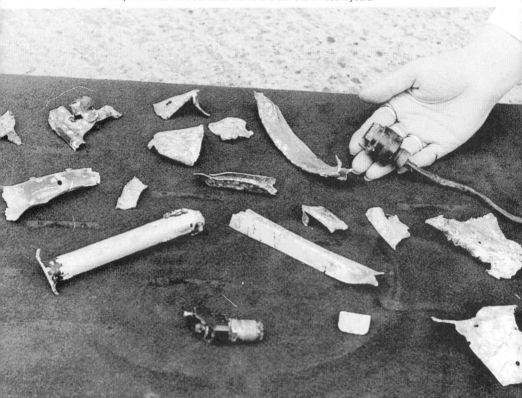

Left: The silver dope-painted fabric of Wellington MF627 with the rear turret missing.

L-20A, Beaver, 26145, 81ST Fighter Bomber Wing, Air Depot Wing, 7519 OPRON, Air Support Group USAF, flying from Sculthorpe to Burtonwood, crashed Bramah Edge, Glossop, 5th December, 1956.

Map reference 056976 ● Map key number 51

Flying an aircraft on instruments is effortless these days when compared to the methods of flight navigation in use 40 years ago. Hundreds of thousands of holiday-makers each year make air journeys with little thought given to the successful navigation of their aircraft. Apart from the occasional trouble with air-traffic controllers or with baggage-handlers, the majority of air travellers today have few problems and a flight to Tenerife is viewed in much the same way as a rail trip to Blackpool was viewed in the 50s.

There can be little doubt that air accidents in the early post-war years served to give impetus to navigational evolution and development. One such accident occured with an American L-20A Beaver—a tragedy which well illustrates the hazards and shortcomings of early radio-navigation systems. This, in combination with pilot error, mis-identification by ground control and adverse weather conditions, all served to bring about the crash on Bramah Edge.

During the 50s Burtonwood (Base Aircraft Depot 1) was the main servicing depot for US squadrons in Europe; in December 1956 a Republic F-84 Thunderjet belonging to 91st Fighter Bomber Squadron, based at Sculthorpe, had been serviced at BAD-1 and was awaiting collection. The pilot assigned to fly the Thunderjet back was 1/Lt Guy Waller; the pilot detailed to take him to Burtonwood in Beaver 26145 was 1/Lt John Rossman Tinklepaugh.

On the morning of the flight 1/Lt Tinklepaugh visited the flight briefing room at Sculthorpe to collect all the relevent information needed to formulate a flight plan. Sergeant Stewart provided him with the weather forecast, which had been made available from 0900 hours that morning. It didn't look good; a cold front was begining to sweep in towards Burtonwood at 15 to 20 knots and the cloud base along the entire route was between 1,200 and 2,500 feet. Visibility was forecast to vary from three to five miles with showers of rain, and consequently Tinklepaugh had to file a flight plan to Sculthorpe Air Traffic Control under Instrument Flight Rules (IFR). This meant that he would be out of sight of the ground all the way, and so unable to map read. He was required to fly over strategically placed radio beacons along a given route.

Each beacon had its own identification signal which was broadcast at 30-second intervals. Along with this, two letters were sent in Morse code—the letter 'A' (dit-dah) and the letter 'N' (dah-dit). The A and N signals were transmitted so that the sounds overlapped each other thus producing a constant tone. When an aircraft drifted either right or left then a distinct A or N signal was heard and the pilot could make a course correction until the constant sound was picked up again. The A and N signal transmission was referred to as a 'radio beam' and was sent out either side of the transmitting tower. When an aircraft passed directly over a radio beacon its radio receiver went quiet, as the signal could not be picked up from that position—this was known as the 'cone of silence'. If, for some reason, the pilot failed to discern that he had passed over the cone of silence, or believed that he had when he hadn't, he had no way

of checking if he was approaching or leaving the transmitting station—the constant A and N signals remained the same on both legs. If unsure of his position he could call up and receive a fix by RDF (radio direction-finding).

With conditions as they were Tinklepaugh submitted a flight plan, but in the event he was directed to make a change. He was instructed to fly first south-west on a short leg so that he passed over Marham Beacon at 4,000 to 4,500, feet and to contact Molesworth Control at Marham as he did so. That meant that Tinklepaugh had to make some re-calculations before take-off. Things started to go wrong from that point.

Air Traffic Control at Sculthorpe had scheduled take off time for 'Air Force 145', Tinklepaugh's Beaver, for 10.25 and yet the aircraft was still at the end of the runway twenty-two minutes later. Why Tinklepaugh failed to take-off at the time scheduled is not known. Certainly those responsible for relaying the weather information at Sculthorpe were unaware of the delay—they were convinced that Air Force 145 had gone as scheduled. Consequently, they did not pass on the updated weather information that became available whilst Tinklepaugh was still on the ground, important information for any aircraft flying IFR. They made no attempt to relay the crucial information by radio because no doubt they believed that Molesworth Control would supply the revised wind changes anyway. What they didn't know was that Tinklepaugh had decided to give that leg of the journey a miss—in the event he never did contact Molesworth as he had been instructed.

As Tinklepaugh and his passenger, Guy Waller, in Air Force 145 headed on the course that had been originally submitted, they encountered headwinds of 50 knots at 280 degrees. Working on the earlier weather information that he

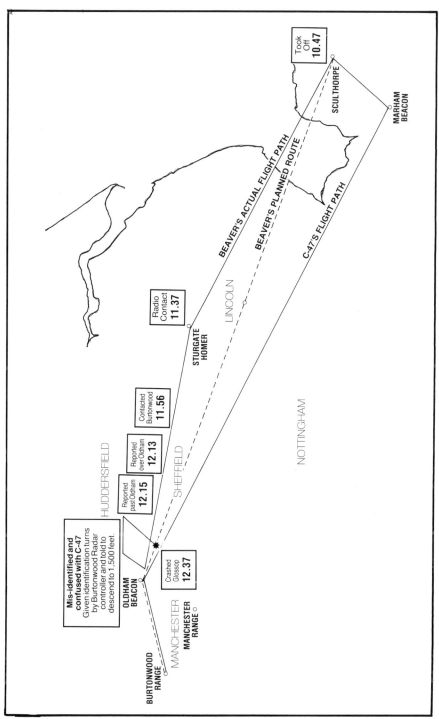

Took Off **10.47**

SCULTHORPE

MARHAM BEACON

BEAVER'S ACTUAL FLIGHT PATH

BEAVER'S PLANNED ROUTE

C-47'S FLIGHT PATH

Radio Contact **11.37**

STURGATE HOMER

LINCOLN

Contacted Burtonwood **11.56**

Reported over Oldham **12.13**

Reported past Oldham **12.15**

HUDDERSFIELD

SHEFFIELD

NOTTINGHAM

Mis-identified and confused with C-47. Given identification turns by Burtonwood Radar controller and told to descend to 1,500 feet.

OLDHAM BEACON

Crashed Glossop **12.37**

MANCHESTER RANGE

BURTONWOOD RANGE

had been given Tinklepaugh was firmly convinced that they were up against a 20-knot wind at 270 degrees, and so believed that they were further along their route than in fact they were. This, along with another factor, served to seal their fate.

Back at Sculthorpe, whilst Air Force 145 was battling against a headwind, a C-47 transport (Dakota) took off at 11.00 with Captain Hill at the controls and a crew of five; they too were heading for Burtonwood. Captain Hill, however, did fly to Marham as instructed—he was also in possession of the correct weather information. He was flying higher and faster and so was catching up on Air Force 145 as both aircraft were converging on the Oldham Beacon (the final transmitting station before the Burtonwood Approach Beam).

Meanwhile, Tinklepaugh, would have been working on the assumption that after a specific period of flying time had passed, he should have reached a certain point along his route. He must have been puzzled when his first contact was with Sturgate Homer at 11.37, a beacon ten miles north-east and five miles behind his intended track; there and then he would have had to revise his course and timing for a new flight-path to the Oldham Beacon.

Twenty minutes later Tinklepaugh attempted to radio Manchester Zone, which controlled all air traffic in the area, but was unable to make contact on 120.3 mcs. He then contacted Burtonwood and gave his position as being east of Oldham Beacon and cruising at 4,500 feet. He asked for and received at that point the correct updated weather information. The significance to his position in the air of that extra 30 knots of headwind must have escaped him. Burtonwood ATC gave him clearance to come in on the Burtonwood Range (that range station was situated some five miles from the runway and was used for approach and landing). He was told to report passing over the Oldham Beacon's cone of silence.

Area Radar Surveillance was provided by Air Traffic Control Unit Antrobus, which was ten miles south of Burtonwood. When Burtonwood radar controllers asked for permission to bring down Air Force 145 to 2,500 feet it was denied by Antrobus. They instructed that because of the high ground in the area, Air Force 145 had to be clearly identified on radar by Burtonwood. It was at that point that the aircraft was turned over to Burtonwood Ground Control Radar.

Identifying and bringing in aircraft by radar was, as has been said, in its infancy, and extremely primitive by today's standards. Before an aircraft could be permitted the use of any form of radar service it had to be properly identified by the controllers. The procedure was for the controller, once he had picked up a 'target' on his screen, to instruct the pilot with whom he had been put in contact to perform a series of course changes; if the blip on the screen was seen to perform the manouevres it was assumed that correct identification had been made, and landing assistance was given. There were dangers, however, and instructions for ground- radar controllers carried the following warning under the heading 'Mis-identification':

*The mis-identification of an aircraft can lead to a hazardous situation in which separation from other aircraft or terrain clearance may be lost. If mis-identification does occur it is usually made by over-confident controllers making assumptions of identity and not carrying out the proper procedure. However, it is possible on rare occasions for mis-identification to occur even if a standard method of identification has been used (this might happen if two aircraft make coincident turns or **if a pilot makes a grossly inaccurate position report which coincides with the position of another aircraft**). Radar controllers should therefore be alert to this possibility and keep a constant watch for any*

Firemen and police survey the tangled wreckage of the Beaver. Far below in the background can be seen Torside Reservoir and the Hadfield-Woodhead Road.

inconsistencies in echo movements or D/F bearings whilst providing radar services.

If a controller discovered that a mis-identification had occured then he was instructed to inform the pilot to carry on under his own navigation. Confusion in this instance was on its way in the shape of the USAF C-47 transport piloted by Captain Hill.

At 12.15 the Beaver, with Tinklepaugh at the controls, reported that he had just passed Oldham Beacon and was inbound for Burtonwood Range flying at 3,500 feet. With that information the radar controller at Burtonwood glanced at his screen sure enough a blip dutifully appeared indicating an inbound target at fourteen miles east-north-east.

"Burtonwood GCA to Air Force 145, turn on heading 225 degrees for identification."

The controller watched for the blip on the screen to begin moving in another direction—it didn't ... a clear case of mis-identification.

"Burtonwood GCA to Air Force 145, continue on to approach beam. Turn on 040 degrees at 3,500 feet. Stand by for weather report ... twenty-one hundred overcast; visibility ten miles; wind, southwest 13 gusting to 20. Altitude setting 29.96."

After the radar controller had made that transmission he immediately picked up another blip on the edge of the screen eleven miles east-south-east of the field on an inbound heading. Believing it to be Air Force 145 he transmitted a course change of 310 degrees—once again the target failed to alter its course. So Tinklepaugh was told to carry on under his own navigation towards Burtonwood Range.

At 12.28 Tinklepaugh reported to Burtonwood GCA that he was over the range station and asked for approach and

ASHTON-U-LYNE REPORTER

Smashed cockpit area and signs of the intensive fire which followed the crash.

landing instructions.

"Burtonwood GCA to Air Force 145, turn on heading 040 degrees."

Two minutes later the controller saw the blip on the screen seemingly carry out the course change—now he had the Beaver on his screen. Or so he thought.

"Burtonwood GCA to Air Force 145, turn on heading 090 degrees."

Once again the blip dutifully obliged.

"Burtonwood GCA to Air Force 145, you are clear to descend to 1,500 feet—report passing 2,000 feet."

Tinklepaugh replied: "This is Air Force 145 inbound for Burtonwood passing through 2,800 feet."

When the target on the screen was six miles east-north-east of the runway the controller called Tinklepaugh and instructed him to turn onto a heading of 225 degrees, then descend to 1,500 feet. The controller watched for that final manouevre on the screen, but it didn't happen.

"Burtonwood GCA to Air Force 145, you have not complied with last instruction."

"Air Force 145 to Burtonwood GCA ... Negative! I am now on heading of 225 degrees."

At once the controller realised that he had a classic case of mis-identification. Obviously the target on his screen that was quite clearly making a standard approach to Burtonwood was not the aircraft with which he was in communication. So where was Air Force 145 making its turns in preparation for

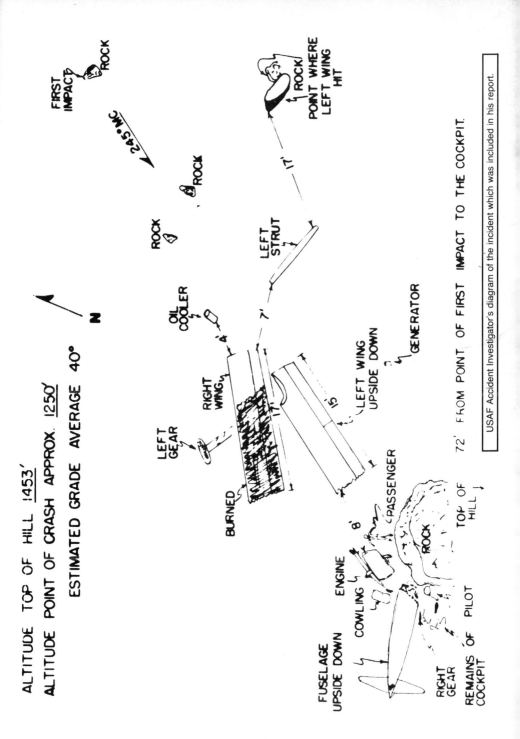

ALTITUDE TOP OF HILL 1453'
ALTITUDE POINT OF CRASH APPROX. 1250'
ESTIMATED GRADE AVERAGE 40°

N

FIRST IMPACT
ROCK

245° MC

ROCK

ROCK

ROCK

POINT WHERE LEFT WING HIT

17'

LEFT STRUT

7'

OIL COOLER

RIGHT WING

LEFT GEAR

BURNED

LEFT WING UPSIDE DOWN

GENERATOR

17'

15'

FUSELAGE UPSIDE DOWN

ENGINE

COWLING

8'

PASSENGER

ROCK

TOP OF HILL

RIGHT GEAR

REMAINS OF PILOT COCKPIT

72' FROM POINT OF FIRST IMPACT TO THE COCKPIT.

USAF Accident Investigator's diagram of the incident which was included in his report.

coming in to land at Burtonwood Air Base?

Quickly the controller called back: "Burtonwood GCA to Air Force 145, climb to 2,000 feet. Advise that you re-home on Burtonwood Range. When you have established your position advise us of your heading—Over!"

The next transmission from Air Force 145 consisted of a single shouted word: "What!" The target that had been mistaken for Tinklepaugh in Air Force 145 faded as Captain Hill in the C-47 dropped below the radar beam and came in to land at Burtonwood.

Leslie Simpson, of Padfield, was manning the Torside signal box when he heard the sound of a single-engined aircraft low in the overcast—it was 12.37. It was then that he heard a dull thud high up on the hillside in the direction of Glossop. The clouds that were shrouding the tops of the hills at a spot known locally as the Devil's Elbow were lit with an orange glow. He put in a call to the emergency services.

A car with two men in it stopped and

MIKE LAWTON

after determining the direction of the crash, set off up the hill, but when they reached the conflagration they could see that nothing could be done.

"We found one of the bodies still in the remains of the cockpit—the other person had been thrown out ... they were badly burnt ... there was nothing that we could do," reported one of the would-be rescuers.

The wreckage was burning furiously and continued to do so for a further 90 minutes.

The following factors contributed to the crash:

1. Tinklepaugh's late take-off.
2. Wrong weather forecast supplied.
3. His failure to fly the recommended route to the Marham Beacon.
4. The C-47 taking-off just 13 minutes later for Burtonwood, but with the correct weather information and following the recommended course over Marham.
5. Tinklepaugh's miscalculation of his position and his informing Burtonwood ATC and GCA of his erroneous positions.
6. The C-47's appearance on the GCA radar operator's screen at the time of Tinklepaugh's radio contact.
7. The radar controller, misled by the information he received, made a mis-identification and instructed the pilot to descend over the hills. Only when it was too late did the controller request Tinklepaugh to seek a radio fix.

Tinklepaugh was twenty-five miles short of where he thought he was—the headwinds being faster than he had originally been informed. His mind must have been fixed upon the time factor and where he ought to have been after 12.00 on his flight path. When he emerged from the clouds he expected to see the ground approaches to Burtonwood rather than the rocks and greenery of the Pennines —hence his final exclamation.

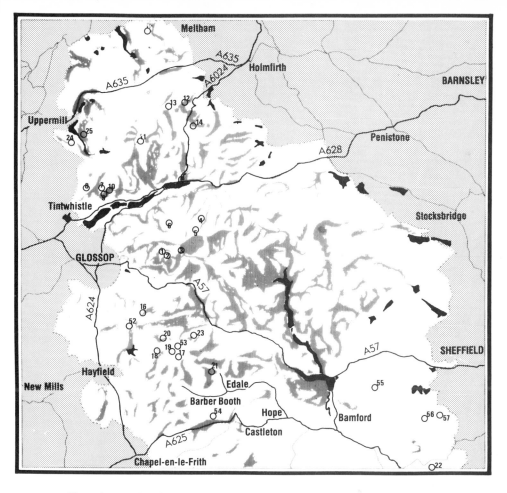

Aircraft crash sites covered in the companion volume, DARK PEAK AIRCRAFT WRECKS Book 1 by Ron Collier:

1 LANCASTER KB993
2 C-47 SKYTRAIN
3 SUPERFORTRESS
4 BOTHA
5 DEFIANT N3378
6 BLENHEIM L1476
7 LANCASTER PA411
8 CHIPMUNK
9 HURRICANES
10 LIGHTNING P38
11 METEORS
12 SABRE RCAF
13 SWORDFISH
14 LIBERATOR 43-94841
15 FLYING FORTRESS
16 SABRES RAF

17 ANSON LN185
18 MILES HAWK
19 HARVARD
20 HAMPDEN AE381
21 HEYFORD
22 WELLINGTON Z8491
23 DRAGON RAPIDE
24 DAKOTA G-AHCY
25 MOSQUITO

52 LIBERATOR 42-52003
53 BLENHEIM Z5870
54 HAMPDEN X3154
55 VAMPIRE XE866
56 WELLINGTON Z8990
57 BLENHEIM Z5746

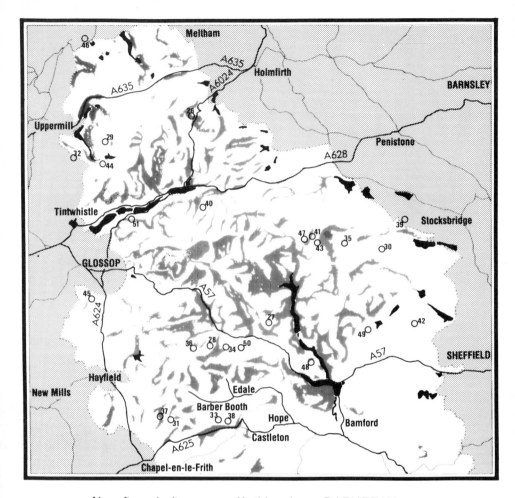

Aircraft crash sites covered in this volume, DARK PEAK
AIRCRAFT WRECKS Book 2 by Ron Collier:

26 HAMPDEN L4055
27 DEFIANT N1766
28 WELLINGTON W5719
29 LYSANDER
30 WELLINGTON DV810
31 THUNDERBOLT
32 LIBERATOR PB4Y
33 SPITFIRE
34 HALIFAX
35 STIRLING
36 ANSON N9853
37 OXFORD HN594
38 OXFORD NM683

39 ANSON N9912
40 WELLINGTON R1011
41 OXFORD LX518
42 WELLINGTON MF627
43 V1 FLYING BOMB
44 TIGER MOTH
45 MUSTANG P51D
46 BARRACUDA MD963
47 CONSUL
48 METEOR RA487
49 VAMPIRE DH100
50 WELLINGTON X3348
51 BEAVER

Mountain Rescue Service

In the Spring of 1943, the Air Ministry received a letter from the USAAF thanking them for the aid given to the pilot of one of their aircraft by the 'RAF Mountain Rescue Service', when the American pilot had survived a crash in the Peak District.

A nice gesture by the Americans, but the Air Ministry didn't know what their allies were talking about. They had no units known as 'Mountain Rescue'. This well illustrates the situation surrounding the origins of the Mountain Rescue Service. Rather than powers at the Air Ministry discerning a need, then directing, organising and equipping a body of men to deal with the effects of a high ground accident, it was more a case of events forcing the birth of such a unit.

The story of mountain rescue in the Peak District began with 28 Maintenance Unit, based at Harpur Hill, Buxton, and the unit's medical officer, the then Flight Lieutenant David Crichton.

Back in 1942 calls became more frequent to Harpur Hill from police and farmers concerning aircraft crashes in the area. 'Doc' Crichton and a couple of RAF medical orderlies would turn out to give what assistance they could with one small ambulance.

Specialised equipment was unheard of and Doc Crichton had to make do with the very basics. As conditions on the hills became more demanding, he was compelled to look around for help, whenever a call came through that there had been a crash. Volunteer helpers were drawn from any RAF personnel who happened to be on hand at the time. Those who made it known that they were prepared to be on call, grew into a small band of dependable volunteers drawn from men of various trades. When a call went out that an aircraft was 'down' they would set out immediately, often after a

hard day's work, to scour the moors; then, next day, they would be back at their jobs after being up all night.

"They were indeed a wonderful lot of chaps," recalled Doc Crichton. "We had no formal training, no special equipment, and certainly no knowledge of mountaineering, so we had to do everything the hard way. Officially, as far as the Air Ministry was concerned, we didn't exist.

"I remember going down to an old retired sailor in Buxton who taught me how to splice ropes."

Experience dictated the equipment needed — and the methods by which that equipment was gradually acquired were better not examined too closely. Similar RAF units in the vicinity of mountainous regions in this country, were likewise being forced into existence by sheer necessity, such as the one at Llandwrog in North Wales.

By the end of 1943, the number of Allied airmen who had lost their lives in crashes on the high ground in the United Kingdom, had risen to a staggering 571. The Air Ministry was convinced.

The hitherto haphazard rescue operations were promptly organised and in January 1944, the RAF Mountain Rescue Service officially came into existence. Specialist equipment along with training suddenly became available for all the volunteers. By the end of 1944 eight teams were in existence and they had attended, up to that time, fifty-four crashes. Out of the two hundred and twenty-six persons involved in the crashes, forty-nine had been rescued alive.

The unit based at Harpur Hill had, by the time of their official recognition, attended upwards of forty crashes. During that period they had 'won', by dubious means, a Jeep, military issue cold weather clothing, stronger boots than regular pattern issue, a rocket gun for sending up flares and walkie-talkie sets.

Some of the necessary equipment was designed and manufactured on the spot by the volunteers themselves. They had discovered, during the course of their operations, that the regular stretcher presented difficulties, so a sledge was designed and built that was better suited for transporting casualties down cliffs and up steep slopes.

In those early days there were hardships and dangers for the volunteers and not just from extreme weather conditions, but from the wrecked aircraft. "We must have been extraordinarily lucky not to have been injured ourselves while extracting casualties from the wreckage," recalled Doc Crichton. "Amongst the twisted metal we encountered bombs, ammunition and also leaking high octane fuel."

The pioneer of the MRS at Harpur Hill, Doc Crichton, left the station in 1946 and eventually retired from the RAF with the rank of Air Commodore. His place at Buxton was taken over by Flight Lieutenant Doc McPherson, followed by Squadron Leader Allen. In 1949 oversight went to Flight Lieutenant Fitton and he left command in 1952.

It was during the immediate post-war period that much was done to improve the MRS. Sophisticated equipment was provided and training courses in rock climbing, winter mountaineering and rescue were introduced for potential team leaders and volunteer members.

The Mountain Rescue Service has been in existence for fifty years, and although the incidence of air crashes has been virtually eliminated by introduction of better aviation equipment, along with safer flying regulations, ramblers still go missing on the moors and climbers are still injured; blizzards can, and still do, trap people in their vehicles on the roads over the mountain tops. The MRS — born out of a need during the war years — still has a place in our time, in the saving of human lives.